John Bowden

What about the Old Testament?

SCM PRESS LTD

SBN 334 01772 6

First published 1969
by SCM Press Ltd
56 Bloomsbury Street London WC1

© *SCM Press Ltd 1969*

Printed in Great Britain by
Billing & Sons Limited
Guildford and London

scm centrebooks

Contents

Contents

Foreword

This book is about the Old Testament. During the course of it, however, we shall be spending quite as much time looking at other people – and ourselves – looking at the Old Testament as we shall spend looking at the Old Testament itself. Even when we concentrate on the Old Testament, we shall also be looking at the world in which it came into being, at the expense of doing proper justice to what is distinctive about the Old Testament and its thought.

This approach has been chosen deliberately, despite its disadvantages. First of all, the Old Testament is there to be read. The *Revised Standard Version* and the *Jerusalem Bible* already offer two very good translations, and it will not be long before the Old Testament part of the *New English Bible* is published. And the Old Testament needs to be read before it is judged. If those who attack it or dismiss it were to read it more carefully, they would find that their arguments would have to be put in a very different way.

Secondly, reading the Old Testament requires background knowledge and historical information if it is to be done properly. Of course, Old Testament scholars have written many books which bring out the meaning of the Old Testament against its background in a way which a small study could not hope to rival. Often, however, consciously or unconsciously, they presuppose not only information but a way of thinking which the non-specialist may not have. And there are not many books which combine some essential details about the Old Testament and discussion of its place in Christianity within a small space.

The present book therefore attempts to cover a great deal in a few pages. It can be no more than the briefest of introductions to a large and complex subject and needs to be supplemented at many points by further reading. But at least it may provide a way in to the enormous field of modern biblical scholarship and its many important studies.

While writing this book I have been made to realize even more how well the study of the Old Testament is served by excellent books. There has been opportunity to list only a few, and I have used the footnotes, apart from justifying my most obvious borrowings, to point out those which are most accessible and most useful for further reading. This means that there are many debts that remain unacknowledged in detail. I hope those to whom they are owed will understand. Two people, however, must be mentioned here. First, Christopher Evans, now Professor in New Testament Studies at King's College, London, without whom I might never have studied theology at all, and who has taught me more than he perhaps realizes; and second, Peter Ackroyd, Samuel Davidson Professor of Old Testament Studies in the University of London, whose scholarly care and advice here, as in much else, has been of immense help. The shortcomings are my own.

Highgate
August 1968

ACKNOWLEDGMENTS

Permission is gratefully acknowledged for the quotations of a passage from *Archaeology and Old Testament Study* edited by D. Winton Thomas, published by Oxford University Press (p. 41); also the passages from *Essays in Old Testament History and Religion* by A. Alt, published by Basil Blackwell (pp. 64, 65).

1 Varieties of Interpretation

Interpretation, asking questions about meaning, seems to become a more intangible and varied business the more one thinks about it. Take the interpretation of anything that can reasonably be regarded as a work of art: a painting, a piece of music, a play, a book. As we look, listen or read, what in fact is it that comes over to us?

A good deal will depend on ourselves: what our make-up is and what our experience is. The more we bring, the more we shall tend to get back. Many things play their part: familiarity with other painting, or music, or theatre, or literature; familiarity with the immediate background and period of a work; knowledge of form and structure; knowledge about the author and his characteristics; more generally, our own experience and sensitivity and insight.

Sometimes the means of communication is indirect and takes place through an interpreter, who has to take decisions in the light of the factors we have just seen when he makes his presentation. A piece of music can be performed in different ways, depending on conductor and orchestra; a play can be presented in a production with a radical change of setting; a poem or a book can be changed in translation.

With all this variety of interpretation and reception, just what is it that is being interpreted? What is the constant at the centre of it all? Clearly there *is* a constant, something objective, but it is harder to define than might appear at first sight. And as to essential meaning – differences between critics are familiar and are not just a matter of perverseness; there is a degree of ambiguity inherent in many works of art which itself provides a basis for alternative interpretations.

These remarks are commonplace enough, and it might be thought that they were concerned with only a secondary matter. Perhaps the question of meaning does not really need to be answered. Can it not be left open? After all, the painting, the music, the play, the poem, is there – and that is the main thing. Yet, on the other hand, surely the purpose of painting, music, literature is to provoke a response; and if it falls short of doing that, then it has, or we have, failed.

Given that point, we can go one stage further: the response can be a legitimate or an illegitimate one. Where the borderline comes is, of course, again a matter for dispute, but it is there to be discussed. And that brings us to the place of criticism, which is especially concerned with all these questions.

The essence of criticism can be summed up in some remarks of a professional critic which not only shed more light on the argument so far, but help to take it further. They are concerned only with literature, but as the present book is at least about a piece of literature, the question of interpretation can now be narrowed to that field:

> The primary critical act is a judgment, the decision that a certain piece of writing has significance and value. It asserts a hold in some way upon my intellect, which entertains the propositions which it makes. It appeals through my senses and imagination to my capacity to recognize order and harmony and to be delighted by them. It appeals also to my experience as a human being, to my conscience and moral life. I put the triad in this order because in literature, whose medium is words, unintelligibility prevents recognition of the presence of either beauty or wisdom. We must feel that the work 'makes sense', even if at first only in patches, if we are to feel its value. But, of course, in experience we are not conscious of these different kinds of value as distinct. It is only for purposes of analysis, and when we come to try to rationalize our responses, that we separate what is in a work of art not separable: what it says, how it says it, and why what it says is important to us.[1]

All this is relevant to an understanding of the Old Testament. Whatever else it is, it is a piece of literature, and it has been reckoned to have significance and value. Problems of interpretation and assessment are more difficult than with other pieces of literature because the unity of the Old Testament is so complex a question. Nevertheless, we can expect literary criticism to illuminate its appeal in some way, for in the case of the Old Testament, too, we are inevitably concerned with answering the three questions with which the above quotation ends: what it says, how it says it, and why what it says is important to us.

So far, we have approached the question of looking at the Old Testament in the categories of literary criticism, but this is to restrict severely the perspectives from which it has been interpreted in the past. Not only is the Old Testament a piece of literature: it is also a Bible (or part of a Bible) and as such has been regarded as a book which contains a pattern to live by, a set of laws to be obeyed.

It therefore also poses the kind of questions which a lawyer has to try to answer in interpreting statutes: questions of application. Just how is the text to be applied? Is it to be interpreted literally, in a timeless sense, as conveying just what its words, taken by themselves, signify? Or has the interpreter to be more liberal, to discover as best he can what the words meant to those who wrote them and then interpret the spirit of them in a very different setting? Christians and Jews have wrestled with these questions for centuries, and the variety of their solutions is still to be seen.

Finally, a third question has been taken into account. Again, in being the Bible (or part of the Bible), the Old Testament has been believed to have a special quality, to be inspired, to have an authority deriving from the fact that it is the word of God. If this premise is accepted, then is the Old Testament perhaps to be interpreted in a special way? May there be more to its message than meets the eye? Does interpretation here call for a special method all its own? Should the interpreter look for hidden meanings, for a special sense to words which in another context might seem ordinary?

We shall have to consider all the questions, directly or indirectly, in one way or another. But an essential preliminary is seeing what the Old Testament itself is and says, and how it came into being. These are historical questions, and they will be historical questions asked in the light of our modern understanding of the world, because this is the way

11

criticism must begin to work. That is not to say that other considerations will not have to be taken into account later. But we must begin historically, in the light of the world as we see it. For the basis of men's communication with each other is the conventional wisdom of a period, presuppositions that are taken to be self-evident. These presuppositions cannot, of course, be seen as final; the boundary between the self-evident and the problematical is extremely fluid. They are, however, vital in that if we depart from this ground without justifying ourselves by argument, it will be impossible to communicate properly and impossible to develop understanding. Our conventional wisdom is dictated by science and history; so what is called scientific historical criticism is unavoidable.[2]

That does not mean that it is easy to apply; the next chapters will show how seriously it can be misused. Asking the right questions is a difficult art. The problem is that the questioner cannot discuss his subject, if it is the Old Testament, in a vacuum. He is tempted always to overestimate the force of his criticism, while those he is trying to persuade will be conditioned by previous attitudes.

These attitudes differ, and are subtly all-pervasive. They linger on, sustained by influences both direct and indirect. Both Judaism and Christianity have had a rich understanding of the Old Testament. In Judaism, the influence of the Old Testament has been direct – on thought and practice and custom and even in being the backbone of a longing for a national state. In Christianity, the influence is more complex: the Old Testament, in a peculiar Christian interpretation, has been a factor in architecture and liturgical dress and ceremonial, in the imagery of hymns and devotional writing and the structure of services. And, of course, it is still read day by day, Sunday by Sunday, in regular services. This background has left its mark.

But the roots of such a use of the Old Testament, in both traditions, lie in a very different understanding of the world from our own; the way in which interpretation of the Old Testament has led to this varied usage goes in unfamiliar stages and by methods which we might even want to call illegitimate. The result of the encounter between the earlier approach and that of the modern world-view was a serious clash, particularly at the beginning of historical criticism, and because this conflict has been and still is such an important factor in understanding criticism, we must do it full justice. A first essential is to look more closely at the way in which the Old Testament was interpreted in the past.

The Old Testament is a Jewish book. It, and it alone, is the Jewish Bible. And it is looked upon with joy as a real treasure. The Jews do not, of course, call it the Old Testament; it is referred to as the Bible, the Law (and the Prophets and the Writings),[3] or by many modern Jewish scholars as the Tanak (the initials of the Hebrew words for Law, Prophets and Writings with vowels to make them pronounceable). As one Jewish scholar puts it:

> In the history of Judaism, the Tanak was continuously accepted as divinely revealed sacred literature. Moreover, for Jews, it represented not only a sacred literature, but also a national, indeed a folk literature. Without a doubt the affection of the Jews for the Tanak allowed them to overlook the bare quality of portions of the writings. Their attitude has been: the Tanak is ours; it is wonderful, and we love it.[4]

These are the words of a man as knowledgeable in biblical criticism as his Christian colleagues, and there is no doubt that the last words express his own feeling, too. A more conservative Jew, with far less use for criticism, says the same thing in different words:

> One cool observer has said that the worship of the Torah is the idolatry of the Jews. It is a sharp half truth. Denied a visible image to worship, denied any divine messenger or prophet on whom to lavish their affection and heap their burdens and supplications, denied any intercessor at all – denied all but the word of God written in a scroll, the Jews have given to that scroll all the loyalty, love and honour that men are capable of.[5]

This attitude could be traced back down the centuries to the beginning of Judaism: we see it in the scribes who so clearly enjoyed their work and saw heaven as a continuation of it, and in the later parts of the Old Testament and Apocrypha, like Psalm 119 and Ecclesiasticus 39. Even

13

Paul, the Christian who rejected the Law, cannot disguise his love for it, so that coming to the conclusion he must about it is agony for him.

To put this attitude to the Old Testament in its context, we have to look not only at the Old Testament itself but also at the way in which it was interpreted and the community through whom the interpretation was done, for all three are very closely bound up together. The core of the Old Testament was the Law, its first five books, attributed to Moses, and from the beginning the Law was presented through interpreters; it is interesting to see that those who rejected this interpretation, the Sadducees, found a focal point elsewhere, in the temple, and when that was finally destroyed their movement died out.

Jewish interpreters took the inspiration of the Law for granted and drew their own conclusions:

> The rabbinical schools had no theory of the mode of prophetic inspiration . . . but it was with them an uncontested axiom that every syllable of Scripture had the verity and authority of the word of God. It followed that the contents of the sacred books were throughout consentaneous, homogeneous. There were not only no contradictions in them but no real differences. The notion of progressive revelation was impossible; the revelation to Moses was complete and final: no other prophet should ever make any innovation in the law.[6]

The other sacred books explained the Law, so a common approach was to use proof texts in threes: a verse from the Law supported by one from the Prophets and a third from the Writings. This was not, as it might seem to be, a question of confirmation, but to show how the Scriptures emphasized God's word by repetition. The use of proof-texts and the emphasis on the special quality of the Law give an indication of the characteristics of this approach:

> The conviction that everywhere in his revelation God is teaching religion, and that the whole of religion is contained in this revelation, is the first principle of Jewish hermeneutics. To discover, elucidate and apply what God thus teaches and enjoins is the task of the scholar as interpreter of Scripture. Together with the principle that in God's revelation no word is without significance, this conception of Scripture leads to an atomistic exegesis which interprets sentences, clauses, phrases, and even single words, independently of the context

of the historical occasion, as divine oracles; combines them with other similar detached utterances; and makes large use of analogy of expressions, often by purely verbal association.[7]

Although it might seem so, this interpretation was not felt to be arbitrary, but to be based on specific principles. Rules of interpretation were laid down; one set of seven principles is ascribed to Hillel, a Rabbi of the first century A D. But the details need not concern us, as the basis on which they are laid down is so completely alien. Nor is it possible to attempt even a brief representative sketch of this Rabbinic exegesis at work; it is too variegated for that. As Judaism before the Christian period was a complex phenomenon and the Rabbinic emphasis was not the only one, we must rather try to bring alternative approaches into the picture at the same time.

Rabbinic interpretation was pragmatic: that is to say, it was concerned with action, with rules for living. If we look at the men who settled at Qumran, by the Dead Sea, to separate themselves from the rest of Judaism and wait in the desert for the end of the world, we find a very different approach. The Qumran sect were also convinced that God spoke through the Old Testament, but they believed that his message consisted in a prediction which was being fulfilled in them and in their time. So sure were they of this, that they did not hesitate to read from (or into) the wording of the Bible their past and present and their expectation for the future. One has only to look at their commentary on the prophetic book of Habakkuk to see the lengths to which this could go.[8]

The Rabbis and the men of Qumran come from a Hebrew language background, but this represents only half of Judaism. Equally important is the Greek-speaking side, for whom the Old Testament had been translated. Legends grew up around this translation (the Septuagint), as around the original, and it, too, was thought to be divinely inspired. One of the most famous Hellenistic Jewish interpreters was Philo of Alexandria, a rich and cultured man with a great interest in philosophy. By his time the principle that the Old Testament need not always be taken literally –

which followed from the Rabbinic approach we saw earlier – came to him as part of Jewish heritage. He took this allegorical approach (for that is what it amounted to) and gave it a philosophical twist. He, too, had rules which he sets out in detail, but again we can look only at the purpose behind them, for the rules themselves are once more based on quite alien presuppositions. He tried to retain the importance of God's law and obedience towards it alongside the outlook of Greek philosophy. The Old Testament stories thus become allegories of the universal and moral laws of nature; Plato, Aristotle and the Stoics in Jewish dress.[9]

Philo was not the first to adopt this method in Judaism, and it also had links with Greek philosophical interpretation of Homer and the ancient Greek myths. (Influence from Greek interpretation is probably to be seen also among the Rabbis, for Hellenistic influence was spread over a wide area at this period.) But as we shall see, he in particular had a great influence, though it was more on Christian interpretation than on later Judaism. The reason for this is that before long the variety of Jewish thought gave way to a much stricter uniformity; for example, Christian use of the Septuagint led the Jews to abandon it for other more accurate, revised versions, and the fall of Jerusalem resulted in the dominance of the Pharisees, who mark the beginning of the great Rabbinical tradition. This work was developed through a varied history down to our own time, but in basic principles it did not depart far from the Rabbinic approach that we have already seen. Along these lines, interpretation was added to interpretation as Judaism came to grips with different historical situations, without there being any significant change in method.

Of course, the rise of modern critical study made a severe impact on Judaism. As in Christianity, it evoked considerable hostility in the slow process of seeking acceptance; now, the divisions of opinion within Judaism are not dissimilar to those to be found in Christianity. But that story is for Jewish scholars to tell.[10] We shall be tracing the development of criticism in Christian circles.

Judaism did, however, avoid one crisis. There never was

and never could be any doubt about the place of the Old Testament in Judaism. In Christianity, on the other hand, along with the rise of criticism came the sharpening of the vexed question of the place of the Old Testament there at all, a question which had been thrust on it from the start and which was given a new urgency as the Old Testament was stripped of what seemed no more than a Christian veneer.

The Old Testament is not, as we have seen, a Christian book. It was taken over, almost fully formed, by Christianity from Judaism. Jesus was a Jew and so were his first followers. In due course the Church broke away from Judaism, but this break was by no means a sudden one. It took a while for the implications of the life and teaching and fate of Jesus to be realized, and for some time the Church continued as a sect within Judaism, part of the greater whole. This period was long enough for the Church to make use of many features of Judaism for its own purpose – often without overmuch questioning – and among the things it took over and retained was the Jewish Bible and with it Jewish methods of interpretation.

There is a good deal of interpretation in the New Testament which is not dissimilar in method to that used at Qumran: the fulfilment of the Old Testament is a theme which pervades the New at all levels. The great difference between the two is the point of reference on which the interpretation rests; for Qumran, the Scriptures pointed to something still to come, while the New Testament writers can already see this crucial point in the past (though more has yet to happen). Similarly, there are also parallels to Rabbinic interpretation. Paul was a Rabbi and he uses Rabbinic methods (as well as predictive allegory) for both theological and practical arguments. (The importance of Jesus is not primarily as an interpreter of Scripture, though many arguments from Scripture are put on his lips; in addition, what knowledge of Jesus is possible through the gospel tradition is itself a separate, and difficult, question.)[11]

Rather later, we can see a fine example of an argument between a Christian and a Jew over the interpretation of

17

Scripture in the *Dialogue with Trypho,* a work written in the middle of the second century by a Christian apologist, Justin. Here we can see a pitched battle not only over interpretation of the Bible but over the text itself; an important matter when two traditions were each using the same work and making rival claims for it.[12]

The methods used by Justin were a regular approach in Christianity until a revolution was brought about, above all by the genius of Origen, the great Christian scholar of Alexandria (AD 185–254), who did pioneer work not only in establishing a good text of the Bible, comparing Christian texts with those used by Jews, both Greek and Hebrew, but also in writing commentaries on entire books of the Old Testament. Interpretation thus became more systematic. Through Origen, Philo's methods of interpretation were to find their way into the Christian Church and remain for more than a thousand years. A statement he makes about his principles is most revealing:

> Wherever in the narrative the accomplishment of some particular deeds did not correspond with the sequence of the intellectual truths, the Scripture wove into the story something which did not happen, occasionally something which could not happen, and occasionally something which might have happened and did not.[13]

Here is a recognition of the difficulty of understanding the Old Testament as Scripture, let alone as Christian Scripture, together with an approach which turns an apparent stumbling block into a divine pointer. God meant the Scriptures to mean something, so if they seem repulsive or meaningless, then they must be read in another way. According to Origen, not all of Scripture had a literal meaning, but throughout it carried a higher meaning. This meaning could be either 'spiritual' or 'moral'.

How Origen's approach worked can be seen quite briefly. An objection came from a certain Apelles that if the ark had really been the size stated in Genesis, it would only have room for four elephants and their food. Origen's retort was that if the measurements are squared all is well, though he was in the end much more concerned with the ark as a symbol for the church.[14] The forty-two small boys who had the temerity to call Elisha 'baldhead' (II Kings 2.23) were only delivered over to 'spiritual' bears.[15] The temptation to laugh is strong. But this sort of approach was also a great positive aid in using the Old Testament as an instrument for teaching Christianity. A passage like the account of the fall of Jericho in Joshua 6 could become powerful preaching:

> Jericho collapsed at the sound of the priests' trumpets. I said before that Jericho is a figure of this world, the power and defences of which are destroyed, as we see, by the priests' trumpets. The world's power and defences, the walls it relied on, were the worship of idols, organized by evil spirits through cunning manipulation of oracles and served by augurs, *haruspices* and magi. All this surrounded the world like mighty walls. The son of Nun, Joshua (Greek: Jesus), foreshadowed the coming of Christ. When Christ came, he sent out his apostles, as Joshua had sent out the priests, and like the priests they carried resonant trumpets, which in this case were the magnificent, heaven-sent doctrines which they preached. The priests blew their trumpets to bring down Jericho. But that was not all. What I find so striking is this. The text says that all the people shouted . . . with great joy. Joy like that seems to me to imply a disposition to concord and harmony of outlook. When such a disposition occurs in any two or three Christians together and they ask their heavenly Father for something in the Saviour's name, he gives it to them. And when there is so much of this joy that in all Christian people there is 'but one heart and one soul', there will be a repetition of the event recorded in the Acts of the Apostles. An earthquake will take place . . . all earthly things will have been destroyed and the world brought to an end.

That is the spiritual sense. In the moral sense, the story also provides advice and instruction in the way of the Christian life:

> We ought all to experience this in our own persons. If you are a priest, make yourselves trumpets from the Holy Scriptures and draw out of them a meaning that can deservedly be called resonant. Sound the trumpet of the psalms and canticles, the prophets and apostles. Carry the Ark of the Covenant seven times round the town by linking the precepts of the gospel with the law. . . . If you succeed, shout for joy, because the world in you will have been brought low.[16]

To say that this method of interpretation continued unchanged until the rise of historical criticism would be a crass over-simplification of a complex and fascinating story which deserves to be known much more thoroughly. But for the purposes of this outline argument, the statement will have to do. There were varieties of interpretation among the Christian Fathers; there were varieties of interpretation through the Middle Ages, as more detailed studies show, but the threefold (or, as became more common later, four-fold) interpretation of Scripture continued.[17] A detailed history of interpretation would have to show times when a more literal understanding of the Old Testament appeared, but they are too sporadic to affect the main point that needs to be made.[18] While there was the possibility of interpreting the Old Testament in an alternative sense, neither the difficulties it presented nor the question of its place in the Christian Church could represent a serious problem.

Before we go further, it is worth pausing for a moment to look at the types of interpretation which have been introduced, both Jewish and Christian, in another perspective. Their backgrounds and histories and methods all differ, but the factor common to them is that here we have various attempts to make a sacred scripture speak to a particular tradition, a particular community. The community provides the interpreters and with them the norms of interpretation (which in Judaism, of course, grow directly out of the scripture itself). The point can be put in an exaggerated way, but not altogether unfairly, in the different case of the Christian Fathers:

On points of Christian doctrine and the faith delivered to the Apostles and communicated by them, they could be earnest, zealous, heroic, even savage and vindictive on occasion; in maintaining the truth of the Gospel they could fill volume after volume with argument and apology; in defence of the faith they lived by and the sacred memorials of their Master they were found ready to undergo contumely, imprisonment, torture, even death itself; but their treatment of the books of the Old Covenant was that of persons whose chief interest in the subject was dependent on the amount of support to be derived from it for their own cause.[19]

The principles of allegory or typology with which Jewish and Christian interpreters worked could not stand up outside the community within which they were used – as was clear to the early Church in its conflict with Gnosticism, for example: that is why they have not been outlined in detail. They can be used to prove anything. The landscape presented by a survey of interpretation from Philo to the Middle Ages and beyond is little short of a world 'through the looking-glass':

> One finds, as did Alice, a country governed by queer laws which the inhabitants oddly regard as rational. In order to understand mediaeval Bible study one must live there long enough to slip into their ways and appreciate the logic of their strict, elaborately fantastic conventions. Philo admits that anything in Scripture may signify any other thing provided that it obeys the rules of an intricate pseudo-science, the allegorical interpretation.[20]

Within the community, it is the life of the community (and in the Church, of course, insights from the New Testament) that is the determining factor in biblical interpretation. Where there is communication with an outside audience, as with Philo, the determining factor is the audience which is sought. Thus while the Fathers speak to the Church and Philo addresses a thought-world of Greek philosophy, the principle is the same.

This situation was inevitable, for what other controls could there be? Science or philosophy had yet to acquire the force they now possess:

> When Aristotle stood against Holy Scripture, it was only a case of one conviction against another. In fact, one conviction based on the authority of a divine revelation stood over against a conviction which claimed for itself an inductively acquired philosophical evidence. Neither of the two positions was demonstrable in the strict sense, nor were they refutable either. It remained a question of decision as to which one took – and it was clear that within Christendom the decision would eventually be made for the authority of revelation.[21]

And who was to be the interpreter of this revelation, Holy Scripture? It had to be the Church and its teachers.

This was changed by the Reformation, of course, but only in one way. The Reformation was primarily a conflict over who should interpret the Scriptures, and did not pose the question of how they should be interpreted in any radically new way. The problem was greater than appeared at first sight. The Church was rejected as interpreter. But what was left? Scripture itself? The Holy Spirit? Luther and Calvin made much of the clarity of Scripture and stressed the primacy of the literal sense, as well as invoking the Holy Spirit, but this, as they and their successors discovered, raised serious difficulties.[22] 'The clarity of Scripture' and 'Scripture its own interpreter' were easier as principles than as practices. The logic of Luther's encounter with the enthusiasts was that more than the Holy Spirit and the Bible itself were needed.

And in a slightly different way, the multiple sense of Scripture was still there. Even Luther read the Old Testament in a 'christological' sense, finding Christ there, and Protestant interpreters in the post-Reformation period found themselves compelled to reintroduce a spiritual sense widely to justify their retention of much of the Old Testament at all.

The real turning-point was not so much with the Reformation, important though that undoubtedly was. To continue the previous quotation:

> The situation had inevitably to alter, the moment that mathematical proof took the place of philosophical evidence acquired by induction. It is no chance that Galileo again and again points out that he does not present a conviction, but stands under a law which goes beyond his personal preference. Only compelling proof gives philosophical truth the priority over theology, and this destroys the old unity of faith and knowledge which was assured by the supremacy of the church authority.[23]

With the arrival of this compelling proof, in the form of the gradual birth of modern science, a crisis arose for the Church, though it was not at first fully realized. As we have seen, although there was conflict between the literal meaning of the Old Testament and the requirements of the present, this conflict could be reduced to a minimum because the interpreters shared the same world-view as the Bible. After all, the biblical world-view was a presupposition of the position from which they interpreted the Old Testament, and any difficulties could be cleared away by methods which they had at their disposal. Now, however, to be able to embrace the Old Testament within the tradition was no longer to prove it true. It had to satisfy other criteria.

Gradually, a different set of presuppositions about the nature and history of the world replaced those provided by the Bible and often came into conflict with the Bible. A second approach to knowledge had appeared, and demanded that the earlier approach be set over against it.[24]

The Reformation took place before this challenge became evident and did not therefore deal with it. The Reformers' world-view was in harmony with the Bible. And before the challenge was recognized, a development in the post-Reformation period had made things worse. By adopting a position in which Scripture had taken the place of the other authorities on which previous Christians had also relied, Protestant scholasticism not only reintroduced a spiritual sense but also began to stress the verbal inspiration of the Bible more than ever before, even taking over arguments discarded by the Jews, in favour of strict verbal inerrancy. As has been hinted, and as we shall see more fully in the next chapter, it was the hardening of fronts represented by this position which made the clash, when it inevitably came, more serious than it need have been.

Before we move on to that, however, one last theme needs to be introduced.

As we saw earlier, there was a tension in Christianity which was absent in Judaism, over the place of the Old Testament in the Church. It began right at the beginning. How new was Christianity, and how much was it a further development continuous with what had gone before? The tradition we have already followed through was conscious of the continuity, and its approach was intended to preserve it. Others, however, historically on the fringes of the Church, took the opposite line. Marcion of Pontus, a second-century figure about whom we know little and whose writings are preserved only in quotations made by his opponents, set the Old Testament in antithesis to the New. He attempted to exclude it, and in the process found it necessary to excise half the New Testament as well. Gnostics, too, were concerned to cut Christianity's roots with the past. That there is not more opposition to the place of the Old Testament until the end of the Middle Ages is probably a result of the Church's control of study and the general inaccessibility of the Bible. With the eighteenth century, however, the conflict flared up again, as the deists used the Old Testament as one more weapon with which to attack traditional Christianity. Thomas Morgan's comment, taken at random, is typical of many:

> The Law of Moses was a miserable system of superstition, blindness and slavery: the Jewish priests deceivers, and the prophets the real originators of the civil wars and disasters that resulted in the doom of Israel and Judah.[25]

The comments of this period are crude and immature, but as study of the Old Testament by critics continued, basically the same sentiments began to be expressed in rather milder language by an increasing number of people. In the nineteenth century this problem, like so many similar ones which arose, caused great agony. Now it has more often than not been left to one side out of apathy, though every now and then a new complaint sparks off a brief controversy. But it is not settled. In practice, the Old Testament is losing its place by default.

Whether or not this is a good thing is the ultimate issue with which we are concerned, but before we consider it we have some way to go. As a next stage, we shall take up the issues raised by this chapter in a different way, by watching more recent interpreters of the Old Testament at work. The starting-point will be England in the mid-nineteenth century.

NOTES

1. Helen Gardner, *The Business of Criticism* (London, 1959), pp. 6f.; the whole book contains a great deal of illuminating comment relevant to biblical criticism.

2. See especially G. Ebeling, 'The Significance of the Critical Historical Method for Church and Theology in Protestantism', in: *Word and Faith* (London and Philadelphia, 1963), pp. 43f.

3. The Law consists of Genesis to Deuteronomy; the Prophets are divided into the Former Prophets (Joshua–II Kings) and the Latter Prophets (Isaiah, Jeremiah, Ezekiel and the Twelve – not Daniel); the rest make up the Writings. See e.g. R. Davidson, *The Old Testament* (London, 1964), pp. 16f.

4. S. Sandmel, *The Hebrew Scriptures* (New York, 1963), p. 526.

5. Herman Wouk, *This is My God* (New York and London, 1960), pp. 182f. The whole book is well worth reading for its picture of Judaism.

6. G. F. Moore, *Judaism*, Vol. I (Harvard, 1927), p. 239.

7. *Judaism* I, p. 248.

8. The text can easily be found in G. Vermes, *The Dead Sea Scrolls in English* (Penguin Books), pp. 235 ff. See the whole section on 'Biblical Interpretation' for the varieties of approach at Qumran.

9. For Philo, see E. R. Goodenough, *An Introduction to Philo Judaeus* (Oxford, 1962).

10. For a brief account see Bernard J. Bamberger, *The Bible: A Modern Jewish Approach* (New York, 1963).

11. See T. G. A. Baker, *What is the New Testament?* (London, 1969). For interpretation of the Old Testament in the New Testament period see R. M. Grant, *A Short History of the Interpretation of the Bible* (New York and London, 1965), pp. 5–71; C. K. Barrett in: D. E. Nineham (ed.), *The Church's Use of the Bible Past and Present* (London, 1963), pp. 1 ff.

12. A convenient translation (abridged) is: R. P. C. Hanson, *Justin's Dialogue with Trypho* (London, 1963).

13. Origen, *De Principiis* IV, 1.15.

14. See H. Chadwick in: *The Church's Use of the Bible*, p. 37.

15. R. P. C. Hanson, *Allegory and Event* (London, 1959), p. 219.

16. Origen, *Homilies on Joshua*, 7.1 f.; quoted in J. Daniélou, *Origen* (London and New York, 1955), pp. 167 ff.

17. See especially Beryl Smalley, *The Study of the Bible in the Middle Ages* (Oxford, 1962).

18. For more details, see the works listed in note 11.

19. E. M. Gray, *Old Testament Criticism, Its Rise and Progress* (New York, 1923), p. 49.

20. *The Study of the Bible in the Middle Ages*, p. 5.

21. K. Scholder, *Ursprünge und Probleme der Bibelkritik im 17. Jahrhundert* (Munich, 1966), p. 116.

22. Incidentally, a point to be considered by those firmly convinced that the Bible needs only to be distributed to speak for itself in Christian terms is provided by a story not widespread in Christian circles. A peasant named Donato Manduzio in the remote Italian village of San Nicandro began to read a Bible he had obtained from a Protestant missionary. He became convinced of the truth of *Judaism* and won many fellow-villagers over. The group was admitted to the Jewish community in 1946, and after Manduzio's death emigrated to Israel. See Bamberger, *The Bible*, p. 9.

23. Scholder, p. 116.

24. For this, see especially G. Ebeling, 'The Critical Historical Method', pp. 46 ff.

25. Thomas Morgan, *The Moral Philosopher* (London, 1738), p. 322.

2 Critics at Work

Saturday, February 7th, 1863, saw the appearance of the first number of the *Church Times*, a sober affair of eight pages, price one penny. Its first editorial, in full-blooded Victorian prose, left no doubt as to its good intentions and lofty aims:

> We shall be found strangers to that narrow party spirit which substitutes sneering and mis-representation for argument and fact. ... On the contrary, while stating our own principles distinctively and without reserve, we shall ever be ready to make full allowance for the honest prejudices and partialities of those whose religious principles have been cast in a mould differing from our own.

This tolerance, however, was not without limits even for so high-minded a paper on its début, and by the end of the last page the style (and the good intentions) had begun to slip. At the end of a column of trivia, including the latest rage in New York – ladies of fashion wearing clerical bands in streets and drawing rooms! – comes a piece of verse presented under the pen-name *Hebraicus*:

> Oh Bishop Colenso,
> You dish up old ends so
> That each ignoramus collates and disputes;
> Just rub out your figures,
> Go back to your niggers,
> And seek not for mare's nests in dry Hebrew roots.
>
> Your Hebrew is bosh,
> It bewilders your *rosh* (Hebrew for head)
> And 'twere better if you had been dum;
> Your teaching is evil,
> An aid to the devil,
> And all your theology ends in a hum.

John William Colenso, first Bishop of Natal, had clearly

fallen very foul of Christian public opinion. Although he was not the first to raise the problem of Old Testament criticism in England,[1] his ecclesiastical position inevitably brought him into the limelight.

To see what lay behind the attack we have to follow Colenso's earlier career and the motives behind his work, which he himself described at some length.

Colenso was trained as a mathematician, and it was as a tutor in mathematics at Cambridge that he first turned his mind to theology. At this stage, and while he worked in an English parish, he did not question current views of the authority and inspiration of the Bible, though he did differ sharply over one question which occupied his contemporaries a great deal, that of eternal punishment. His first theological book, on the Epistle to the Romans, caused considerable concern because it seemed to challenge the doctrine, and the attitudes of his opponents to this earlier work certainly coloured their views on what he was to write later.

In 1853 Colenso went out to Natal as its first bishop, and amidst a great deal of other activity set out to translate the Bible for the Zulus, thus making acquaintance with the Old Testament in the most thorough way in which it is possible to know a document. He soon found himself up against great difficulties, which he set out in a letter to an English professor of divinity, though, for reasons which we shall see, the letter was never sent:

It has happened that I have been brought again face to face with questions which caused me some uneasiness in former days, but with respect to which I was then enabled to satisfy my mind sufficiently for practical purposes, and I had fondly hoped to have laid the ghosts of them at last for ever. Engrossed with parochial and other work in England I did what probably many other clergymen have done under similar circumstances. I contented myself with silencing ... the ordinary objections against the historical character of the early portions of the Old Testament and settled down into a willing acquiescence in the general truth of the narrative, whatever difficulties might still hang about particular portions of it. If a passage of the Old Testament formed at any time the subject of a sermon, it was easy to draw from it practical lessons of daily life, without examining closely into the historical truth of the narrative.[2]

The work of translation, however, brought him face to face with the questions he had put by. While he was translating the story of the flood and discussing the rendering with one of his Zulu helpers, Colenso was asked whether it was all really true. Colenso's knowledge of geology alone made him unable to answer positively, and he had to prevaricate. Another Zulu began to challenge the morality of the Old Testament, pointing out that it seemed to be in no way superior to the folk tales of his own people. Yet another made the tension unbearable:

> I shall never forget the revulsion of feeling, with which a very intelligent Christian native, with whose help I was translating these words ['And if a man smite his servant, or his maid, with a rod, and he die under his hand; he shall be surely punished. Notwithstanding, if he continue a day or two, he shall not be punished; for he is his money'] into the Zulu tongue, first heard them as words said to be uttered by the same great and gracious Being, whom I was teaching him to trust in and adore. His whole soul revolted against the notion that the Great and Blessed God, the Merciful Father of all mankind, would speak of a servant or maid as mere 'money', and allow a horrible crime to go unpunished, because the victim of the brutal usage had survived a few hours.[3]

But still Colenso hoped that this was a difficulty which could be resolved.

He pursued the problem with a vigour that was characteristic of all that he did. He read all the traditional and conservative answers, together with the new studies being carried on in Germany, 'both the bane and the antidote'. His letter to Oxford was part of this search. But there was no easy solution. All the traditional approaches seemed evasive to the point of offensiveness, and even the learned Germans used their erudition to obscure the issues. There was nothing for it but to press on with his own original investigation, aided in his calculations by his past mathematical training. Before long, doubts had changed to certainties and the letter to Oxford asking for enlightenment never went off. The reason: even though it might be possible to get round the stories of the creation, the fall and the flood by allegory, or some other expedient, the narrative of the Exodus, 'whatever value it may have, is not historically true'. And this was not 'a doubtful matter of speculation at all; it is a simple question of facts'.

The facts were set out over a long period, from 1862 onwards, in a five-volume work, *The Pentateuch and the Book of Joshua Critically Examined*, the prefaces to which give a running commentary on the debate as it proceeded with the theologians and bishops of the Church. Colenso made his one point with a pedestrian, unimaginative and dogged sameness. The facts as stated in the Old Testament narrative of the first five books of the Bible just could not be true; and as this was a simple matter of fact, what was the Church of England, which by law required subscription to them as true, going to do about it?

The Old Testament states that six hundred thousand able-bodied men left Egypt at the Exodus, implying a total population of at least two million. How could such a force be got away in a single night? 'Remembering, as I do, the confusion in my own small household of thirty or forty persons, when once we were obliged to fly at dead of night . . . I do not hesitate to declare this statement to be utterly incredible and impossible.'[4] The host of two million gives Colenso the time of his life in offering comparisons. What of the sick and infirm, or women in recent and imminent childbirth, in a population like that of London, where the births are 264 a day, or about one every five minutes? How can one imagine the whole congregation on the march, as a body twenty miles long and six yards wide? The whole story reaches the heights of absurdity in the sacrificial regulations, according to which the animals at the passover would have to be killed at the rate of 1,250 lambs a minute and each priest would have had to sprinkle the blood of 333 lambs a minute for two hours together. Finally:

We have to imagine the Priest having himself to carry, on his back on foot, from St Paul's to the outskirts of the Metropolis, the 'skin, and flesh, and head, and legs, and inwards, and dung, even the whole bullock'. . . . Further, we have to imagine half a million of men going out daily, the 22,000 Levites for a distance of *six miles* – to the suburbs for the common necessities of nature![5]

Similar considerations, applied steadily over the first six

29

books of the Bible, occupy Colenso for some thousands of pages.

There was more to Colenso's pedestrian labours than meets the eye. Throughout, his motives were the same as those behind his work on the Epistle to the Romans. He was disturbed at apparent dishonesty at the heart of the Church and at the hindrance that the difficulties which he stressed placed in the way of the preaching of the Christian Gospel. He himself was ready, if need be, to relinquish his episcopal orders, but as what he had discovered was, after all, a matter of fact, he had hopes of a happier outcome:

It may be that the time is near at hand ... when the way shall be opened for a wide extension of Missionary work among the heathen, when that work, which cannot make progress either among the ignorant Zulu or the learned Hindoo, shall no longer be impeded by the necessity of our laying down, at the very outset, stories like these for their reception and requiring them, upon pain of eternal misery, to 'believe' in them all 'unfeignedly'. ... How much better to open wide the door and let in the blessed light and air of day into every part of our spiritual dwelling! That light indeed may show us that the stories of the six days' creation, the Noachian deluge, the slaughter of 68,000 Midianitish women and children, are no longer to be spoken of as historical facts. We may perceive that it is no longer possible to confound the early legends of the Hebrew people, and statements contrary to reason and the facts of nature, or condemned by our moral sense. ... What a day of regenerated life will it be for the Church of England, when these things shall be spoken of plainly and freely in every pulpit in the land, when the Bible shall be opened and the story of its origin explained and the real value of its histories discussed, as the records of living men, like ourselves, written down by living men.[6]

As a critic, Colenso has little more than curiosity value. His work has made no lasting contribution to the study of the Old Testament. In the sphere of Old Testament study he was an amateur rather than a professional; he came to the discipline late and the work he did was only one part of a varied and distinguished intellectual activity, which was itself only one facet of a full life, in which people and practical issues were constantly in the foreground. Nevertheless, he is a good person with whom to begin a look at criticism, as he points up some of the most important issues more sharply than others more learned than he was.

As will have become evident, what Colenso lacked most of all was a historical sense. If the Old Testament had the character he thought that he had discovered, how did it get that way? Having made his basic point, why did he not content himself with a few examples and then go on to some more constructive work? But before we are too hard on Colenso, we have to remember two things. First, that a sense of history is something which has been developed in us above all over the last hundred years, so that it has grown up alongside the process of criticism and, secondly, that Colenso was driven to the great lengths of his detailed argument by the terms on which his opponents took up his challenge.

Colenso quotes two opinions which further investigation will show to be quite representative of the time:

If the belief in the infallibility of the Scripture be a falsehood, the Church founded upon it must be a living fraud; . . . in all consistent reason, we must accept the whole of the inspired autographs or reject the whole, as from end to end unauthoritative and worthless.

The Bible cannot be less than verbally inspired. Every word, every syllable, every letter is just what it would be, had God spoken from heaven without any human intervention. . . . Every scientific statement is infallibly accurate, all its history and narrations of every kind are without any inaccuracy.[7]

These statements, the first from a Boyle Lecturer speaking in Oxford in 1862, and the other from Baylee's *Verbal Inspiration*, a manual used by those preparing for ordination, show the stakes involved. In an argument in these terms there is simply no room for history and historical development.

And on these terms, Colenso convincingly wins the day. At least his books still stand as a refutation of simple fundamentalism. If they are read! But they were not read, even in his own day. What mattered then was simply what he had said, not how or why he had said it. He had apparently broken his ordination vows and so the consequences were the ecclesiastical ones of deposition and excommunication by the Bishop of Cape Town (though this was not upheld in the English courts), censure by the English bishops accompanied by widespread hostility and personal vindictiveness, and attempts at the first Lambeth Conference to secure more effective action against him through the Anglican Communion. All this by men who did not hesitate to admit that they had not read what he had written.

It is also true that Colenso's opponents had some justification for their reaction, if not for the ways in which it was expressed, for Colenso seems set on excluding a great deal of the Old Testament from the Church. Despite his disclaimers to the contrary, the logic of his position seems to lead to the conclusion that the Old Testament is historically and morally untrustworthy, and should therefore be out of the way. He does little to bring out the 'glories' to which he occasionally does lip service. A negative attitude of this kind can ultimately be no more than a parody, and the hurt reactions of bishops and professors of divinity are not least expressions of the fact that something important has been forgotten, even if their detailed arguments suggest that they have a long way to go before they see what the 'something' is.

The case of Colenso is not the only example of the bad reception given to criticism, and the after-effects of these battles have lingered ever since. There is more to criticism than the asking of questions which are raised by a simple reading of the Old Testament. The fact that the Bible occupies its special place in the Christian Church and a Christian civilization, and that questioning it touches on beliefs by which people live, brings added difficulties. The right to criticize has been won through an immense amount of human sacrifice, in terms of impeachment for heresy, dismissal from academic office, personal abuse and ridicule, even leading to death. Colenso here is only one of a considerable company.

Nor is even the dispute in which he was involved a thing of the past. The disturbing thing is that more than a century later, arguments can still be carried on in the same unhistorical way on the same narrow front, with the same barrenness. For what really emerges from the type of controversy in which Colenso was engaged is that it is not argument about the Old Testament, which is never really allowed to speak in its own right, but about a principle – about the nature of a holy book and the question whether the Old Testament is one.

For the Old Testament to make sense, as we have already been arguing, there is need for a sympathetic historical understanding of its contents, including a knowledge of the way in which it was put together. Again, if Colenso had known more of the nature of the sources behind the books he analysed, a great many of his difficulties would have vanished immediately.

The imagination, historical insight and constructive and systematic questioning which Colenso failed to apply were brought to bear soon after on the Continent by a professional who devoted his whole life almost exclusively to biblical studies, and a look at his way of working will make this quite clear. The scholar concerned is recognized as one of the greatest scholars of the nineteenth century and he was, like so many of them, a German, Julius Wellhausen. But even his approach was attacked by the Church of his day.

Wellhausen was nineteen at the time of the Colenso controversy, but only nine years later he had been installed as professor in one of the great German universities among which he was to spend his long life until he died in 1918. Whereas Colenso had been in essence a rationalist, concerned only with figures and accuracy and possibilities and impossibilities, Wellhausen was interested in the living process of history. After being disappointed in the lectures of some of the great names in German theology in his undergraduate days, he was attracted by the vivid quality of the lectures of the famous Heinrich Ewald to make Old Testament study his field. Such was his success, that his chief contribution during the first part of his life was to turn the Old Testament, as most earlier scholars and others, Christian and Jew, knew it, literally upside down.[8]

He, too, tells his own story, in the preface to his *Prolego-*

mena to the History of Israel, published in 1883. He describes graphically how it all began:

> In my early student days, I was attracted by the stories of Saul and David, Ahab and Elijah; the discourses of Amos and Isaiah laid strong hold on me, and I read myself well into the prophetic and historical books of the Old Testament. Thanks to such aids as were accessible to me, I even considered that I understood them tolerably, but at the same time was troubled with a bad conscience, as if I were beginning with the roof instead of the foundation; for I had no thorough acquaintance with the Law, of which I was accustomed to be told that it was the basis and postulate of the whole literature. At last I took courage and made my way through Exodus, Leviticus and Numbers. . . . But it was in vain that I looked for the light which was to be shed from this source on the historical and prophetical books. On the contrary, my enjoyment of the latter was marred by the Law; it did not bring them any nearer me, but intruded itself uneasily, like a ghost that makes a noise indeed, but is not visible and really effects nothing.[9]

The difficulty was that if the biblical account was right, Saul, David, Ahab and Elijah should be obeying the law reported as having been given by God to Moses, the law to be found in the first five books of the Old Testament. According to this law, sacrifices should be being offered only in Jerusalem, and according to definite laws of ritual, not as and where and how men chose. But even where there were points of contact, there were also differences, all the difference, in fact, between two wholly separate worlds.

Light came unexpectedly, as it often does, from a chance meeting. In conversation with the great systematic theologian Albrecht Ritschl, in Göttingen, Wellhausen learnt of a scholar who had argued that the books attributed to Moses were in fact to be placed later than the time of Saul, David and the prophets. Without knowing the reasons for this view, Wellhausen was quite prepared to accept it. Once again he went through the first five books of the Old Testament and confirmed to his own satisfaction that they were not written by Moses at the start of the history of Israel, but were made up of four different documents, each coming from a different period. Each document was written in a sufficiently distinctive style for it to be possible to identify large stretches of it once the search had begun.

And instead of being a work by a single author, written before 1000 BC, the Pentateuch was shown to be a composite volume, formed over almost five centuries, from the ninth century to the fifth century BC.

Of course, Wellhausen drew on the work of predecessors who stretch back into the eighteenth century, but the full development of the new theory was his own. That it was unpopular goes without saying. Its effect in Jewish circles was like that of radical gospel criticism in the Christian Church, and Christians were equally concerned. For now, instead of having a divine history leading through Law and Prophets to the coming of Christ, the Old Testament was seen to come to a climax in legalistic Judaism.

Nor was this all. There were pessimistic historical conclusions to be drawn from the theory, which Wellhausen himself was not slow to point out. If all the different documents were written long after the events they describe, then we have no reliable information about these events, but 'only of the time when the stories about them arose in the Israelite people; this later age is here unconsciously projected, in its inner and its outward features, into hoar antiquity, and is reflected there like a glorious mirage'.[10] We know nothing about the patriarchs and very little indeed about Moses.

All this inevitably tended to reduce Wellhausen's estimation of the importance of the Old Testament. The patriarchal period was too hazy for us to know anything about, and its customs must in any case have been primitive ones; the law was largely late and ritualistic, a decline from the highest point of Old Testament history. All that was left of real interest was the prophetic movement, which Wellhausen, like so many of his contemporaries, saw in nineteenth-century dress – great inspired individuals, motivated above all by a concern for right and wrong. Here, he felt, was the key to the Old Testament.

The attacks made on Wellhausen by the Church disturbed him very considerably and in 1882 drove him to take a decisive step. His letter to the Prussian Minister of Cultus shows his position vividly:

35

Your Excellency will perhaps remember that in Easter 1880 I requested, if it were at all possible, to be transferred into the Faculty of Philosophy. At the same time, I tried to set out the reasons for my request. I became a theologian because I was interested in the academic study of the Bible. It then gradually dawned on me that a professor of theology also has the practical task of preparing students for ministry in the Protestant Church, and that I was not up to this practical task. Despite every restraint on my part, I was making my pupils more unsuitable for it. Since then, my theological professorship has been a heavy burden on my conscience.[11]

He left his chair at Greifswald in the same year and went as a mere lecturer in Semitic studies to Halle; it was three years before he became a professor again, and then only after a bitter struggle.

Here again, an attempt to provide an explanation for what seemed obvious facts brought about immense tension between scholarship and the Church. Again, the problem is that on closer study the Old Testament was being claimed to be something other than it had been thought to be. And again, the Church made no attempt to consider the detailed questions raised. Of course, Wellhausen had no right to be as confident as he was about the results of his study – the Old Testament is more than a crossword puzzle to be set aside when the solution has been found, which is the impression Wellhausen sometimes gives – and we shall see that his results were by no means as final as he thought. Nevertheless, this is criticism which can only be made with hindsight. And a problem similar to that posed by Colenso, now made even more acute, remains: on careful reading the Old Testament looks less and less like a sacred book for Christianity. Does it really have a place in the Church?

Posed in Wellhausen's terms, the question is a particularly difficult one, but fortunately we do not need to answer it now. An answer can wait until the last chapter, when we have had a chance to look at the Old Testament in more detail. Meanwhile, a change takes place which was to bring Old Testament study to a third, more creative, stage.

Wellhausen was forced out of Old Testament studies by the pressure of church comment, but even had he remained in a theological faculty it seems unlikely that he would have continued to devote himself entirely to the Old Testament. His work bears many marks of finality. Once he had arranged the Old Testament in its new chronological order and shown how this changed the traditional picture of the history of Israel, Wellhausen, like so many of his nineteenth-century contemporaries, seems to have felt that he had brought yet one more problem to a satisfactory conclusion. Others could do the detailed work that remained. Half seriously, half in jest, Wellhausen remarked to a New Testament colleague, 'I'm getting rather tired of the Old Testament'. In the last years of his life he concentrated more and more on Arabic studies and, finally, on the New Testament.

In a way, Wellhausen was right about the significance of his achievement. For he represents a climax in a particular type of criticism, that of putting questions to the Old Testament and trying to find answers on the basis of the information which the text itself provided. Wellhausen was certainly a historian; there is no doubt about that. But he was a philological, literary-critical historian. One of the strangest features of his brilliant academic work is the way in which he failed to consider the new evidence emerging from archaeological discoveries which were to shed so much new light on the problems he had considered. Yet this was the vital factor that was to change the whole appearance of Old Testament studies and to question many of the assumptions which he had made. It was to transform discussions about a book into discussions about a people and a world.

Wellhausen and his contemporaries had been trying to see this world as it were with a guttering candle. Most nineteenth-century scholars knew very little about the background against which the Old Testament is to be set, as there was next to no material available. Abraham, Isaac and Jacob were virtually the first-known historical figures, emerging from the mists of time. The only way of supplementing what the Bible had to say was by analogy. The Bedouins of Arabia, relatively untouched by the development of civilization, were a favourite point of comparison, but the net was spread much wider to primitive peoples of all cultures, to 'the Indians of North America . . . Mexicans, Australians, Shilluk negroes, Kaffir Ashantis, Hottentots and Turks', as one authority put it. Oddly enough, relatively little use was made of the neighbouring civilizations of Mesopotamia and Egypt, as they were thought to represent too advanced a stage for the beginnings of the Israelite people, Occasionally the classical world of Greece and Rome served to provide a parallel for later periods. And along with all this went various artificial ideas of development, analogies from natural growth, progress from the simple to the more complex, and so on.[12]

The result of this was once again an emphasis on the crudeness and simplicity of the Old Testament; it was still impossible to make it come to life in a detailed historical and cultural setting, and the context in which it was viewed was inevitably more or less artificial. Although the Palestine Exploration Fund and other similar bodies were founded in the 1860s, and chance discoveries of considerable importance, like the Moabite Stone, were made in Palestine during the nineteenth century, it was not until 1900 that archaeology began to make extensive contributions.

The false conclusions drawn by archaeologists looking too hastily for confirmation of the biblical narratives, like Sir Leonard Woolley's claim to have discovered evidence for the Flood, belong to a history of biblical archaeology rather than here. What concerns us most is the way in which Old Testament study was quite radically changed. It was as though the candle was replaced by a bright light. The ancient Near East proved to harbour an almost inexhaustible fund of archaeological evidence to illuminate the Old Testament. The most recent and most publicized discoveries, of the Qumran community and its scrolls by the Dead Sea and of the fortress of Masada and its last heroic stand, will immediately spring to mind, but these are only two out of hundreds of discoveries which changed scholars' minds all over again and have kept changing them. Mari, Nuzi, Ugarit, Lachish, Hazor, Jericho and Shechem are only a handful of the important sites which have produced material of various kinds.[13] Even in the past ten years, our knowledge of the Old Testament in its Near Eastern setting has been changed out of all recognition, and many more developments can be expected. For much has been discovered which has yet to be properly assessed, and even more work has yet to be started. One estimate is that only two per cent of potential archaeological sites in the Near East have yet been thoroughly examined.

We are no longer dependent on comparisons and analogies; we have writings, physical remains of buildings, sacred vessels, and everyday objects to give substance to our descriptions. We can see how mistaken it is to compare the patriarchs with primitive peoples of other continents when the period from which they come had already seen the fall of ancient civilizations; we can see just how considerable were the achievements of, say, a David and a Solomon. And – outside the immediate history of the Israelites – Egyptians, Babylonians, Assyrians, Hittites, Canaanites all take on their distinctive features so that we can begin to read their thoughts and follow their beliefs and practices.

Thus after the two earlier stages of criticism at which we have been looking, Colenso's rather primitive attack on the accuracy and morality of the Old Testament and Wellhausen's literary-historical analysis, we have now reached a third stage, the stage in which modern Old Testament study is carried on. As we shall be looking at this in much more detail, there is no need for a particular illustration here; it is, however, important that we should not forget the lessons that the earlier stages have to teach.

The Colenso affair can serve as an illustration, carried to the extreme, of two important points. First, we should be very conscious of the dangers of the frame of mind which is concerned with proving the Old Testament, with justifying it, with showing it to be right. To adopt this attitude has been a recurrent temptation since the growth of archaeological study. There seems to be a widespread feeling that archaeology can 'prove' or 'disprove' the Old Testament. Complete books have been written with this purpose. Prove, say, by archaeology – the argument seems to go – that the circumstances pictured in the Bible are those of the time in which a story is set, and the story is true (and the significance attached to the story also holds). The case is not put quite as baldly as that, but that is what it seems to add up to.[14] The argument is, of course, flawed, and the next chapter will show what it fails to take into account. But quite apart from over-estimating the competence of archaeology, it is a thoroughly bad argument because it is still framed in terms of substantiating a holy book. And at this stage, we are not concerned with the question what we are to make of the Old Testament. We are here not to confirm or to judge, but to understand. And that is rather a different thing.

The second point is very closely connected with this. It is fatal for the question of the relevance of the Old Testament to the present time to be introduced prematurely. Of course, it needs to be raised, but not in such a way as to affect the course of the investigation. In Colenso's comments, we can detect the feeling that the Old Testament should have a status worthy of divine revelation to the age in which the interpreter is living. The answer expected from it is, in one way or the other, required to be a direct one. And as it cannot be a plain yes, then it has to be an equally plain no. The Old Testament is being set against a standard, and an alien one at that.

Once again, however, understanding does not involve value judgments of this kind. It is a neutral approach, which allows the evidence to speak for itself. Of course, its implications may be of immense importance. But they come later. We find exactly the same kind of problem in the famous 'Quest of the Historical Jesus' during the nineteenth century, where the historical investigation into 'Jesus as he was' was entangled with the search for a figure capable of sustaining Christianity. The fault may have been inevitable in the nineteenth century, but there is no reason why we should make the same mistake now.

Wellhausen and his work point to a rather different conclusion, but one which is equally important, and that is the need for open-endedness in biblical study, the need to realize that new discoveries may change the scene quite radically and that therefore there is no room for dogmatism. This is true both in the field of archaeology and in Old Testament criticism, and the point is so important that I make no apologies for introducing a substantial quotation from a recent article:

As soon as an archaeological discovery is made, the problem of its interpretation at once arises. And concerning material which needs to be interpreted there must always and inevitably be differences of opinion. It should cause no surprise, therefore, that there can be, and frequently is, as much disagreement amongst archaeologists concerning the material they study – concerning the character of an object, its value as evidence, its relationship to other archaeological material, its purpose and date – as there is among specialists in other fields of study. It is accordingly as fallacious to affirm that 'archaeology says', as if archaeologists always speak with once voice, as it is to affirm, for example, that 'psychology says', as if different schools of psychology do not exist. Both statements are entirely without foundation. . . . Archaeological evidence is often fragmentary and disconnected, and is only clothed with significance when the archaeologist has given his interpretation of it. Vigorous debate and divergence of view among archaeologists will, and in the nature of the case, must accordingly continue, and few final conclusions must be looked for. Anything like universal agreement will be the exception rather than the rule. The interpretation of archaeological material does not stand still. It calls for constant reinterpretation, particularly in the light of new material that is continually being unearthed. . . . The archaeological situation as seen today can easily be changed, and changed radically, by tomorrow's discoveries. And tomorrow's discoveries, even if they could by good fortune cast new light on old problems, almost always raise new ones, and thus present a fresh challenge to the interpreter.
 The point may next be made that it is not only archaeological evidence which stands in need of interpretation and reinterpretation. The Old Testament itself must be interpreted and reinterpreted on the basis of the most recent research into it, and, as has been said and as is well known, many and varied interpretations are put upon it. These two kinds of evidence – the internal evidence of the Old Testament and the external evidence of archaeology – thus both need to be interpreted and reinterpreted, and the different use of the two types of evidence sometimes leads to very different views concerning problems which are central to Old Testament study.[15]

This brings us to the last question with which this chapter is concerned. As can already be seen, to enter into the world of modern scholarship, in the Old Testament as elsewhere, is to enter into a debate. It is to enter a highly technical discussion between specialists with an extremely high degree of training and with an immense background of reading and study. In this open field of discussion even the apparently most unlikely solutions are given a fair hearing, analysed carefully, tested and assessed, before a final decision is made. The books of these scholars are studded with long footnotes, discussing subsidiary points in the writings of others and giving the evidence for their own conclusions.

In all this lies the safety factor in biblical criticism. Here is the immediate answer to general questions like, 'If it happened so long ago, how can we know that it is true?' 'What if the books of the Bible are all forgeries?' Questions like this, unless pursued, have no force at all other than to indicate the questioner's real reluctance to commit himself to even a cursory study of the evidence. There may be times when the personal convictions of one particular scholar lead him to favour a conclusion rather against the odds, but the open debate, where no argument is spared, means that any palpably false conclusions would long ago have been uncovered for what they were. The vast majority of issues under discussion can claim at least some degree of plausibility.

All the same, the variety and complexity of this open debate is all very confusing, especially to the newcomer. When two scholars differ radically, each producing a mass of learned evidence for his conclusion, which viewpoint is the uninitiated to choose? Is he to favour the approach which seems to fit in best with the other views he is forming? The dangers of prejudice are obvious. Will he perhaps cast a rather sceptical glance at the range of possible solutions and decide that with so much disagreement no one has much chance of being right and that the best thing to do is to steer clear of the critical enterprise altogether? Students who begin to study biblical criticism in the universities often feel this way, so it is to be expected even more of those without so much time at their disposal.

There is justice in this way of thinking, and it is quite true that the variety in patterns of approach and conclusions can be bewildering. But in view of the nature of the evidence, it is hard to see how things could be otherwise. On the other hand, before pessimism sets in, it should be stressed that there are no more problems here than we would expect in any equivalent area of historical reconstruction. Provided that, like historians in other fields, we are willing to forgo 'proof' and 'justification' of the Bible and accept the answer 'not proven' or 'don't know', even at points where our curiosity is most burning, we can acquire a general picture which would satisfy the requirements of normal canons of history writing. Details will change, but provided that we are clear how we reached the picture in the first place and clear about the standing of the picture once we have formed it, adjustment should not be too difficult.

So having watched the critics at work, we can go on to engage in the business directly ourselves.

NOTES

1. Samuel Davidson, an Irish biblical scholar, had been forced to resign from a Manchester college in 1857 for his views on the Old Testament.

2. J. W. Colenso, *The Pentateuch and the Book of Joshua Critically Examined*, Vol. I (London, 1862), p. vi.

3. Colenso, p. 9.   4. Colenso, p. 61.   5. Colenso, p. 40.

6. Colenso, p. 149.   7. Colenso, Vol. II (1863), pp. x, xii.

8. H.-J. Kraus, *Geschichte der historisch-kritischen Erforschung des Alten Testaments* (Neukirchen, 1956), pp. 235 ff.

9. J. Wellhausen, *Prolegomena to the History of Ancient Israel* (paperback: Cleveland and New York, 1957), p. 3. See also W. Zimmerli, *The Law and the Prophets* (Oxford, 1965), ch. 3.

10. Wellhausen, p. 319.

11. Kraus, pp. 236f.

12. See L. Perlitt, *Vatke und Wellhausen* (Berlin, 1965), pp. 80ff., 164 ff.

13. For a magnificent survey of the present state of archaeological exploration, see D. Winton Thomas (ed.), *Archaeology and Old Testament Study* (Oxford, 1967).

14. For an important discussion of this point, see D. E. Nineham, *The Church's Use of the Bible* (London, 1963), pp. 154ff.

15. D. Winton Thomas, *Archaeology and Old Testament Study*, pp. xxiiif.

3 The World of the Wise

It is fatally easy, as teachers will know, to acquire know-ledge about the Old Testament at second hand, without coming to grips with what it actually says. Having looked all too briefly at the immediate background to modern criticism, we must therefore turn directly to the Old Testament itself to examine it quite closely. It is impossible to understand those who write about it without having some idea of the problems with which they have to cope.

But suppose we take up the Old Testament, where are we to begin? The experiences of Colenso and Wellhausen have already brought out some of the difficulties which follow from a straight reading of the text, just as the first chapter warned us that if we fail to take the Old Testament on its own terms we will completely miss what it has to say.

All these difficulties would seem to rule out the possibility of an approach to the Old Testament as we now have it 'on the flat'. It would be very difficult to argue that it has a particular message to us which can be taken in isolation. What gets in the way is the manner in which our minds naturally work. They function very differently from the minds of those whose labours have gone into the writing of the Old Testament. Whether we are conscious of it or not, we are too deeply affected by the developments of the scientific understanding of the world and the gap between ourselves and the past not to need to ask questions. And if these questions are not to be crude, we have seen that they must be governed by a *historical* understanding. We therefore have to set out, in reading the Old Testament, to explore the way in which it grew into its present form.

As the process of development within what is now the Old Testament lasted over a period of a thousand years and saw the rise and decline of Israel as a great nation, with vast changes in social and cultural conditions, this is not an easy task. The process of unravelling the way in which the Old Testament took shape is an immensely complicated one, in which details must inevitably remain obscure and sometimes represent little more than guesswork. As we shall see in more detail in a moment, the people from whose history the Old Testament comes were always interested in the past for what it could say to the present, and this interest governed the way in which the Old Testament has been put together. Traditions, memories, records from the past, in oral or written form, were altered, expanded, put into a new context time and again by later generations, concerned that the message they contained should remain alive for a new age.

Many of the characteristics of this process are agreed by most scholars, and it is worth seeing briefly what they are.

As we saw when we were looking at the work of Julius Wellhausen, scholars no longer regard Moses as the author of the first five books of the Old Testament which have for so long been attributed to him. By and large, the recognition that four different elements go to make up the Pentateuch, as it is called, still stands, and the periods to which Wellhausen assigned these elements are accepted as being not too far out. On the other hand, the elements are no longer thought of in so rigid a form as documents, nor are scholars so sceptical about the historical value of the material which even the latest elements in the Pentateuch contain. The way in which the Pentateuch was formed is seen as a fluid process extending well beyond the decisive periods at which the different elements were combined. Because of the interplay between oral tradition and written material, which is extremely difficult to analyse in detail, a more neutral word than 'document', like 'stratum' or 'tradition', is usually preferred.

The last and final layer, providing the framework for the Pentateuch as we now have it, is thought to have been added in the sixth century BC, though because of the fluid nature of the tradition (see above) this was not a final stage and there are signs that additions were made even after this. We should also regard the material within this layer as having been collected over a considerable period. It is usually called the Priestly Writing. Within that framework, though quite clearly distinct from it, lies a second element, the book of Deuteronomy. This again grew up over a period and was probably completed after the exile. Most scholars, however, would see as its core a book reported (in II Kings 22) as having been found in the Jerusalem temple before the exile, in 621 BC, with contents going back even before that. As we shall see, Deuteronomy has many affinities with the 'historical books' of the Old Testament, so it is often taken with them rather than with the Pentateuch. Finally, still within the framework, we can detect what are usually taken to be two traditions from an earlier date. These derive their names, J ('Jahwist', now usually Yahwist) and E (Elohist), from the Hebrew names they use for God. Separating them is more difficult, and there is much ground for disagreement, particularly about the contribution of the Elohist. Some would see his work as a full-scale narrative dovetailed into that of the Yahwist; others deny it any independent existence. With J, however, we can be reasonably sure that we are going back to a tradition collected and shaped during the reigns of David and Solomon. And once again, it has a great deal of earlier material going back considerably further than that.

How scholars reach these conclusions and how the Pentateuch can be analysed in this way is beyond the scope of the present book, and more detailed knowledge will not be necessary to follow the argument. Those who are interested, however, may like to follow up the question in one of the many clear accounts that have been given.[1] The consequences of these discoveries are fairly easy to see. The process of dovetailing was not carried on without alteration to the earlier material involved, and the motive behind it was not to present a more accurate history of what had happened but rather to interpret the tradition so that it spoke to a given present situation. The provision of a new context for a narrative in itself reinterprets that narrative. Asking historical questions of this material is therefore a very tricky business.

Very similar problems are also presented by the prophets. If we wish to form a historical picture of what the prophets were saying against the background of their own time, once again the tendency to read – and alter – the past in the light of the present gets in our way.

It is extremely unlikely that any of the prophetic books as we now possess them consists entirely of sayings of the prophet whose name it bears. The prophets themselves, Amos and Hosea, Isaiah, Jeremiah, Ezekiel and the rest, were not writers of large prophetic books. Their oracles seem to have been very much immediate comments on the situation of their day. But because these comments were made in the light of a profound understanding of the nature of Israelite faith, they were preserved beyond the time of the prophet. Exactly how this was done is not clear – perhaps some of the material was written down in smaller collections, or else it may have been memorized and handed down orally by followers or disciples of the prophet. It may have waited for a particular crisis before it was collected. Whatever happened, however, was not the exact preservation of the words of a particular historical person. As the situation changed, so the original message could be altered by the addition of new material, by explanatory phrases, by rearrangement.[2] The concluding stages of this process seem to have taken place after the exile, when the future looked much more promising, which may well have brought about a considerable shift in the emphasis in the prophets' words. The problem is typical of many with which the Old Testament confronts us.

Before the exile, the prophets are concerned to make clear the doom with which the nation they address is faced unless it changes its ways. But did they also hold out a positive message of hope? There are certainly 'happy endings' which have been added to a number of the prophecies of judgment and many of them come from the post-exilic period. But do they all? To adopt a sweeping judgment one way or the other is far too hasty; complex questions of style and vocabulary and thought have to be assessed if progress is to be made and they demand a very balanced judgment – the situation is not dissimilar to that which faces us when we try to see what Jesus originally said and what was attributed to him later by the early Church.

There are also the 'historical books'. If the problems here are slightly fewer, they are still difficult enough. 'Historical' may be the adjective which has regularly come to be applied to the books from Joshua to II Kings, but it is worth remembering that Judaism puts them in a very different category. In the Jewish Bible they are the Former Prophets – the important thing, in other words, is that they contain prophecy. They are associated with what we would think of as the real prophetical books as comment on and interpretation of Israelite life in the light of the Torah, the Law. Once again, therefore, we have to remember that they represent a view of the past in the light of a particular present, and that they are not straightforward history writing.

The present in the light of which they were written is the period of the exile; as we have seen, they are closely connected with the composition of the book of Deuteronomy. This means that we have an approach to the past coloured by the fall of Jerusalem and also the destruction of the independent northern kingdom of Israel which occurred in 721 BC. As there was always tension between north and south, and the north was looked on with particular disfavour by the dominant spokesmen in Jerusalem, we may expect less than justice to be done to the history and religious life of the northern kingdom. But equally, the fall of Jerusalem itself must have had an almost traumatic effect on those who experienced it, and we may also expect to find condemnation of what was seen later to have led up to it.

That this has indeed happened is all too plain. The historical books have been edited from a particular theological standpoint which has also probably exercised a degree of censorship. Fortunately for our immediate purpose the degree of editorial activity varies. Where this activity is heaviest, in the latter stages of the historical development of the Israelite monarchy, it is very difficult to achieve a proper historical understanding, and in the books of Joshua and Judges we have to cope with much the same problems as those which arose in the case of the Pentateuch. During the rise of Saul and David and over into the reign of Solomon, however, the editorial work is much lighter, though even here the presentation is by no means simple, as we shall see. Nevertheless, here is the most promising place to begin.

Before we do so, however, one more possible misunderstanding needs to be cleared out of the way, even at the risk of seeming to delay discussion of the actual text interminably. In finding a suitable starting-point we have had to look negatively at a good deal of Old Testament material, and some of its contents have not been mentioned at all. This is only a preliminary step. The aim at present is to see the Old Testament against a historical background, and to do that we have to build up some reliable historical knowledge. Only then can we understand the character and significance of what the Old Testament contains. We shall therefore be coming back at a later stage to look in a different light at much of the material we have temporarily dismissed, and will be looking also at other books which have still to be mentioned.

It will be a help to the reader now to put this book aside and to read the passage at which we have arrived, say, beginning with I Samuel 8 and ending with I Kings 11, in a modern translation and perhaps with a short commentary to clarify any obscure points.[3] In this section we have an account of the reigns of the first three kings of Israel. We see the beginning of the monarchy under Saul, the problems with which he has to deal and the setbacks he experiences, ending with his own death. David progresses towards the throne and by his brilliant leadership is able to defeat the Philistines and establish a large empire in Palestine with a state capital in Jerusalem. There is then a vivid account of the struggle over who shall succeed to the throne of David which ends with Solomon's victory. And, finally, there is a detailed account of the magnificence of Solomon's reign and the way in which he was able to develop a rich and sophisticated society on the foundations which David had provided.

There is plenty here to get our teeth into, and the period covered is relatively short – probably round about a century. Certainly there are few other periods in Old Testament history where the sources are so full. Nevertheless, after all the questioning with which we began this chapter, it is clearly necessary to begin by asking about the value of this particular section of history. This is not a matter of being over-critical; any historian given an account of the past cannot simply accept it as being handed to him on a plate; he has to submit it to his own questioning.[4]

Perceptive readers will have noticed that the material differs quite considerably from place to place and that the account is not completely coherent. In the early stages there are several duplications. There seem to be different attitudes to the establishing of the monarchy (compare e.g. I Sam. 8, 9 and the first half of 10, and 11). There are two descriptions of the way in which Saul is rejected; David is twice introduced to Saul; twice he spares Saul's life. Here we seem to have a combination of different sources. At the end, too, there is also a variety of material. The last four chapters of II Samuel look rather like an appendix to the book, and II Kings 3–11, which describes the reign of Solomon, is also composed of a mixture of passages: I Kings 11.41 mentions a 'book of the acts of Solomon' which probably served as a source for some of the account – but in the final verses in which this book is mentioned we can see the style of the later editor very plainly, and a detailed study would show his influence elsewhere in the material. This is where his activity becomes more marked.[5]

In the middle, from II Samuel 9 to 20, and again in I Kings 1 and 2, we have something noticeably different. There is what is obviously a continuous narrative describing the struggle over the succession to David's throne, which on any count is a masterpiece. As one Old Testament scholar has summed it up:

The supreme historical treasure of Samuel is the Court History. This document stands midway between the old traditional material, with its accretions from popular lore, and the reflective, increasingly doctrinaire histories of later times. It has the factual accuracy of contemporary chronicle. But, unlike the mere annalist, the writer reveals the relationship of character with event, and of one event with another, by the sheer skill of his narration. In the whole of the Old Testament, only the work of the Yahwist is comparable with the superbly simple prose of the Court History. As history, it is unequalled in ancient Hebrew literature. At this period, and for centuries afterwards, the neighbouring civilizations produced nothing comparable. The writer had seen history made in David's reign; and when, probably in the reign of Solomon, he wrote his narrative, he himself made literary history.[6]

The quality of the Succession Narrative is unquestionable. But is its historical character? Have we really found some firm ground on which to place our feet? At this point we come up against one of the scholarly arguments which were mentioned at the end of the previous chapter, and it is not an abstruse one, but of considerable importance.

The view just quoted has long been an accepted one. But a recent work has argued – quite convincingly – that far from having a straight historical account here we have a brilliant combination of propagandist political writing and moral and religious instruction. In short, instead of history we have a kind of historical novel. And the nature of its writing introduces us to the area from which this chapter takes its title – the world of the wise.[7]

To describe the world of the wise, and to point out the characteristics of the Succession Narrative, it will be necessary to take for granted a good deal of critical historical work on this period and describe the world in which the account was written. This rather circular process should then enable us to see the work with new eyes.

Until the rise of Saul, the Israelites lived in the hill-country of Palestine, organized as a loose tribal alliance which we shall be examining more closely in the next chapter. They did not have control over the more populous settled areas because of their lack of resources and inadequate leadership, and it seems to have been in an attempt to better their precarious position that Saul was appointed king. But whatever the exact story which lies behind the present account, he was unable to provide the necessary leadership and was eventually defeated and killed by the Philistines.

It was during the latter part of Saul's reign that David came into prominence, again under circumstances which are not completely clear. David came from Judah, a tribe which closer acquaintance with Israelite history will show to have stood somewhat apart from the main group of tribes, and after his break with Saul he cultivated relations with Judah and its chief city, Hebron. (His desertion to the Philistines is perhaps easier to understand in this light – standing to this extent apart from the rest of Israel, his treachery would not have been as great as it might seem.) After Saul's death, David moved into Hebron and was there appointed king over the clans which made up the tribe of Judah; Saul's surviving son Eshbaal was anointed king of the tribes of Israel in Saul's stead. Eshbaal ruled only two years before being murdered by two of his officers; with his death the way was open for David to become king of all Israel, and not of Judah only. He was more successful than Saul in bringing unity to the tribes and also managed to defeat the Philistines who attempted to stop this new development. His victories removed the Philistine threat once and for all and brought David freedom of movement and a considerable degree of control over a wide area of Palestine. As a final step towards strengthening his position he captured (apparently intact) the ancient Jebusite city of Jerusalem with his own troops and made it his capital. The result was that he became ruler of a powerful independent empire in Palestine, and he was able to devote most of the rest of his reign to consolidating his success and extending the area of Israelite control. His successor, Solomon, was able to go even further in developing the resources of the empire, though the tension between Israel and Judah, the two kingdoms of which it was made up, carried within it the makings of the downfall of the united kingdom which was soon to take place.[8]

The consequences of this acquisition of power were considerable. David was now responsible not only for the rule of a group of tribes settled in part of Palestine, but for a sizeable area of the country, including the original Canaanite inhabitants. A chain of city-states was added to the old tribal pattern. And for the regulation and government of this complex empire a system of professional administration was needed. Whereas Saul's less significant position had led to little change in earlier patterns of life, David's meteoric rise to power made necessary the development of a court and ruling officials along the lines of the other empires of his day. How much was achieved in David's time and how much had to wait for Solomon is not always clear, but this is undoubtedly what happened before long.

Within the short space of time available it was clearly impossible to develop a distinctively Israelite administration from scratch, even if that had been thought desirable, so considerable borrowings were made. There were doubtless suitable officials in Jerusalem and elsewhere in Canaan who had been associated with earlier régimes, but for patterns of training – and help – the natural place to turn to was Egypt, which had many points of contact with Palestine at this period. Lists of officials from David's court include one high ranking officer with an Egyptian name, and titles of positions run parallel to those to be found in the Egyptian court.[9]

Now the relevance of this is that developments of this kind were not purely political. They had religious significance, as we shall see in the case of the king in particular, and they had vast cultural significance, for they helped to bring about nothing less than a new way of looking at the world.

In Egypt, civil administration was a way of life which marked out those involved in it from the rest of the country. To be a scribe was to belong to the privileged, relatively leisured and cultured class, possessing special knowledge and skill, the basis of which was the ability to read and write.[10] There were 'wisdom schools' responsible for training, which imparted not only practical skills but a whole attitude to life:

> In addition to reading, writing and other rudiments the pupil was taught the rules for success and happiness in life which were the product of the experience of many generations. No distinction was

made between the prudential and the ethical, the religious and the secular, the social good and the individual good. Human life was seen as a whole, and in every situation there was a right and a wrong way of behaving, which led respectively to happiness and disaster, to life and death.[11]

In the administrative sphere, education was completed in a government department where the student had a more senior official as his tutor. As in any civil service training, the object of the education would be to produce officials capable of handling complex practical matters of administration with maturity and insight.[12] But this whole way of thought was not solely directed towards administration. Being a way of looking at life, it spilled over to affect all other areas of life, too. Such an attitude also led to an interest in the natural world and human nature for their own sakes – this is reflected in the description of Solomon's 'wisdom' in I Kings 4.30ff., where

He spoke of trees, from the cedar that is in Lebanon to the hyssop that grows out of the wall; he spoke also of beasts, and of birds, and of reptiles, and of fish (I Kings 4.33).

The Israelites, coming out of a much more uncultured background, with a much more restricted view of the world, were confronted suddenly with this different way of viewing experience. Of course, it would not be wholly strange – it was by no means limited to schools and administrators and wise men:

It was the common way of thought and speech, in which those who were called wise excelled. It was an approach to reality. Saying all these things comes close to calling it a philosophy, which it was not; but it dealt with some questions which philosophy also handles, and as a technique of discourse it served the purpose which philosophical discursive reasoning served in Greek thought. The parallel should not be drawn closely; wisdom belonged to everyone, while discursive reasoning was the skill of the intellectual.[13]

We find 'wisdom' in Israelite material which antedates the time of David and Solomon. But the degree of the change, the impact made by new circumstances, amounted to what scholars have described as an 'enlightenment'.[14] And of course this affected earlier religious attitudes. There is a complex process of interaction here which it is impossible to trace in detail in a book like this, but one more quotation will bring out the main point.

> Now for the first time it was possible to understand God's activity in an all-embracing sense. It is no longer seen as something which operates from time to time through the charisma of a chosen leader, but as a much more constant, much more widely embracing factor concealed in the whole breadth of secular affairs, and pervading every single sphere of human life.[15]

It is this approach which lies behind the Succession Narrative, and it is with that in mind that we can finally return to it.[16]

Like the rest of the Old Testament, the Succession Narrative sees the events it describes taking place in the sight of God and under the control of God. But this control is seen as being exercised in a particularly subtle way. It happens through the thoughts and plans and actions of men. There is a tension here, as there is a tension throughout the thought of the wise; they believed that certain types of action led to certain consequences, good to good and evil to evil; but at the same time they were too perceptive not to notice that there was also an imponderable element in human fortunes, and that often the divine control could bring totally unforeseen results which were beyond human understanding.

Nevertheless, despite this latter recognition, the stress is on what happens through *man's* wisdom and counsel, and the closer one looks the more clearly the Succession Narrative is an illustration, on a grand scale, of the precepts of the world of the wise.

Wisdom can be found, in precept form, in the book of Proverbs. Like the other Old Testament books we have been discussing, its material dates from over a wide period and has been altered in the interpretation, but it is only necessary to read, say, Proverbs 16 and 25–27 to have some point of comparison. The Succession Narrative takes these precepts and shows them embodied in real characters in real situations, public and private. Its author was able, through the medium of an account of part of David's reign, to present a wide variety of examples both to be followed and to be avoided. At the same time, of course, he also gave expression to the other element in wisdom that we have noted, the hidden working of God. All this affected his presentation.

There were clearly limits to the degree to which the author could depart from the facts. After all, many of the people he describes were figures of very recent history. But we know enough about political biography to realize that he would have had some scope for invention; we must not forget the other aspect of the work, which was mentioned briefly at an earlier point: the Succession Narrative is also a piece of political propaganda, justifying Solomon's claim to be the true successor to David in a situation where this claim may well have still been disputed. But details of this aspect cannot be discussed more fully here.

In looking at the Succession Narrative, then, we have been able both to form a picture of the Israelite court at the time of David and Solomon and to obtain a rather deeper insight into part of the Old Testament. Nevertheless, the Succession Narrative would not have deserved all this attention had it been the only work of its kind in the Old Testament. But it is not. The period in which it was written also saw the gathering together and reinterpretation of the traditions describing the way in which the people of Israel had reached their present position, in the work of the Yahwist(s).

These writers (or writer – the name is only a symbol for the authorship of the work with which we are concerned) come from the same background as the author of the Succession Narrative. They are confronted with a much larger question. Why are things as they are? What is Israel? Who is the God whom Israel worships and how did he come to be the God of Israel? How was it that Israel occupies the new position which had so recently been reached?

To answer these questions they had a wide assortment of tribal and clan traditions, of legends from various and even unknown sources, and some mythological material. This material could simply have been compiled and transcribed as it stood. Evidently it was assembled by a much more complex process, which we have not yet traced.

Perhaps we have not understood the process because we have forgotten that these were wise men as well as scribes. Their general purpose was to answer the questions set forth above, and what they did can usually be understood in the light of these questions. As wise men they were convinced of the validity of experience; and they knew that wisdom arose from reflection on experience.

We must begin where they began; and they seem to have begun with the belief that Israel was the creature of Yahweh, and that the history of Israel must be the recital of the act of Yahweh. What Yahweh is they could learn by what Yahweh had said and by what Yahweh had done. It was obvious that Yahweh acted with a purpose; and all that had gone into the creation of Israel must reflect this purpose. Plainly not all of the material which they had clearly reflected this purpose; indeed, it is possible that very little of it did. But reflection on the human condition made it clear that this purpose could be discerned. The wise men began with a faith which was not the product of wisdom; it was the product of the collective experience of Israel and its ancestors, and it was the function of wisdom to reflect upon this collective experience and draw conclusions for life. Hence they felt justified in conceiving and in formulating the traditions at their disposal in such a way that the insight of experience was reflected.[17]

We have only to read the stories of the patriarchs, Abraham, Isaac and Jacob, with the delineation of human features and human relationships there to see how the Yahwist writing developed old material in a new way. Here is no history writing as we know it, but there is not complete arbitrariness either. It is the past seen in the light of the present and the present in the light of the past, and all fused together under the conviction of experience.

This beginning made in the tenth century BC is going to be of great significance for later history. But before we follow future developments forward, we have to look back at the past. Our questions will be same as those posed by the Yahwist: What is Israel? Who is the God whom Israel worships and how did he come to be the God of Israel? But we think in a very different way from the Yahwist, and so the way in which we look for our answers will inevitably be different, too.

NOTES

1. See, for instance, G. W. Anderson, *A Critical Introduction to the Old Testament* (London, 1959), pp. 19ff.

2. For an analysis of the construction of the prophetic books see J. Lindblom, *Prophecy in Ancient Israel* (Oxford, 1962), pp. 220ff.

3. For example, W. McKane in the Torch Bible Commentaries, on *I & II Samuel* (London, 1963).

4. See, among others, R. G. Collingwood, *The Idea of History* (London, 1946), p. 256.

5. See Anderson, pp. 72ff.

6. Anderson, p. 80.

7. For more details on wisdom see especially R. N. Whybray, *The Succession Narrative* (London, 1968).

8. See John Bright, *A History of Israel* (London and Philadelphia, 1960), pp. 163ff.

9. See R. de Vaux, *Ancient Israel* (London and New York, 1961), pp. 127ff.

10. See R. N. Whybray, *Wisdom in Proverbs* (London, 1965), pp. 16f.

11. Whybray, p. 17.

12. See W. McKane, *Prophets and Wise Men* (London, 1965), p. 45.

13. J. L. McKenzie, 'Reflections on Wisdom', *Journal of Biblical Literature* LXXXVI, 1967, pp. 2f.

14. So G. von Rad, e.g. 'The Joseph Narrative and Ancient Wisdom', in: *The Problem of the Hexateuch* (London, 1966), p. 293.

15. G. von Rad, 'The Beginnings of Historical Writing in Ancient Israel', *Problem of the Hexateuch*, p. 204; quoted in R. N. Whybray, *The Succession Narrative*, p. 5.

16. For the following details, see R. N. Whybray, *The Succession Narrative*.

17. J. L. McKenzie, 'Reflections on Wisdom', pp. 5f.

4   Memories of the Past

The work of the Yahwist, as we saw it at the end of the previous chapter, was an explanation of the present situation of Israel, for the construction of which a considerable assortment of local, clan and tribal legends of differing origins was available. A tribute to the way in which a reasonable unity was made out of this diverse material is the readiness with which we accept – until it is argued otherwise – the stages which are made to lead from the beginning to the time of David. More likely than not, however, we shall not have learnt this sequence immediately from the text of the Old Testament; at best our knowledge is likely to come from extracts from the earlier books of the Bible, and it is more probable that our knowledge will be in some way at second-hand, from a more popular version.

First comes a gigantic backcloth which depicts the creation of the world by God, a universal flood and a consequent new start, and man's sinfulness emerging once again in the building of the tower of Babel and the scattering of the nations. After this, the centre of interest is focused on one man, Abraham, whom God summons to Palestine from Ur of the Chaldeans. We hear of Abraham's activities in Palestine and have some brief accounts of his son Isaac, a more shadowy figure; with Jacob the narrative becomes more extensive. One of Jacob's twelve sons, Joseph, is sold into Egypt as a slave as a result of a plot by his brothers, but he rises to high office and is eventually joined in Egypt by his father and other brothers. A change of rule leads to great hardships but, under a new leader, Moses, the descendants of Jacob are miraculously delivered from their slavery. They encounter the God who has delivered them at Mount Sinai, where they receive a new law, and after a long

59

period of wandering in the desert they take possession of their allotted territories in the promised land under Moses' successor Joshua. Once in Palestine the tribes experience considerable vicissitudes. From time to time they are oppressed by foreign invaders, and are only saved by the intervention of God, who raises up a deliverer for them. This period of the Judges is followed by the appearance of an important figure, Samuel, who anoints the first king.

Of course, all this outline does not come from the hand of the Yahwist, though it is likely that his work once covered the same period. Later parts of it may have been suppressed with the addition of other interpretations from other hands. Nevertheless, this is the period we have to illuminate.

Alternative courses are open to us. By far the easiest would be to accept this familiar outline as a basis and to look at it in the light of the latest archaeological discoveries. We could adopt as a principle that tradition can be quite reliable and that the outline is to be accepted as it stands unless there is very weighty proof to the contrary.

But before we do that, it is surely not unreasonable to ask how far we should trust tradition. It is very important to see that this is a different type of question from the one which was answered in the negative by Wellhausen. The alternative is not between taking the tradition as giving us reliable historical information or regarding it as being too far away from the events it describes to do us any good. We now have archaeology to show how pessimistic Wellhausen was, and how much ancient memory has been preserved. But we must be aware of the danger of swinging in the other direction and being too credulous. Once again, our examination of the Succession Narrative has pointed to snags which may lie in the way.

This is not being mistrustful. It is essentially a question of being open and working in a proper way. It cannot be said too often that the attitude of trust which a biblical scholar adopts towards his material is a complex one, that he is always aware of the possibilities of error and the need which may arise for him to revise his estimates in the light of new evidence. We are not being excessively sceptical when we feel unable to take the Old Testament account at face value without further ado.

Whatever the difficulties, however, one thing is quite clear. Trust or scepticism will finally be built up only on a study of the details of what the Old Testament actually says, after careful reading and thinking which tries to take all the relevant evidence into account.

Now we only have to read sections of the Old Testament between Genesis and Judges as they stand to see the immense complexity of the material in which our familiar story is embedded. The setting, the persons involved, the type of material change constantly; we have narratives, some fragmentary and some of greater length, social and ritual legislation, poetry, myth, anecdotes, official lists. And everywhere there is the work of later editors, the Yahwist and his successors, so that we have to take possible alterations into account and live with a constant uncertainty over how to date particular sections.

In view of this, an alternative course seems preferable: to try to trace the past history of Israel on as broad a base as possible and building in as many safeguards as are practicable. We cannot hope to sort out all the early material or put it in sequence, so beginning at the beginning is impracticable. Instead, we have to try to work backwards into the past from the reasonably firm ground which we already have.

The Israel over which Saul was appointed king was an alliance of tribes, apparently twelve in number. His task was to bring them greater union, so that they could make a more effective defence against the Philistines, as we saw in the previous chapter. This means that the footing held by the tribes in Palestine was not particularly secure, and both biblical and archaeological evidence seems to confirm this point. The association between the tribes was a relatively loose one, to which modern scholars have given the Greek name 'amphictyony'.[1]

We have fairly extensive knowledge of the Greek amphictyonies, the most important of which was the Amphictyonic

61

League organized around the temple of Demeter at Anthela, near Thermopylae. In its earliest form it consisted of twelve tribes which met in assembly twice a year and was primarily responsible for the maintenance of a central shrine. At the same time, however, the amphictyony had political significance and an amphictyonic oath prohibited certain offensive actions between members.[2] About the Israelite amphictyony we know much less; it is difficult to point to clear arguments in support of its existence. The pattern of the amphictyony is, however, the most illuminating hypothesis that has yet been advanced to explain the nature of the tribal alliance in Israel, and if we accept it as a model, many details from the early Old Testament material slip into place. We find lists of twelve Aramaean tribes in Genesis 22.20–24; twelve Ishmaelite tribes in Genesis 25.13–16 and twelve Edomite tribes in Genesis 36.10–14, which suggests that this form was by no means unique to Israel in the Near East.

The number twelve is unlikely to be fortuitous and is probably dictated by the need for a monthly turn of duty at the central shrine. The place of the central shrine seems to have varied; it was probably first at Shechem, then at Bethel, later at Gilgal and finally at Shiloh. The shrine itself, however, was almost certainly the ark, a small wooden box or chest probably containing tablets of the law. On the religious side there was probably a regular festival attended by representatives of the tribes, to celebrate the covenant which bound the alliance to its God; the tribes would also have been involved politically with each other, though the amphictyony, like its Greek counterpart, was not a political structure. Perhaps its most important political aspect was the Holy War: stories in Joshua, Judges and I Samuel suggest that members of the amphictyony appealed to others for aid when they were threatened from outside (though whether or not the appeal was heeded was a different matter). Many scholars argue that this 'Holy War' was a purely defensive operation, but that is open to question: the line between defensive and offensive war is seldom easy to draw and not all the operations reported fit the defensive pattern easily.[3]

It is difficult to say much more than this about the amphictyony without being misleading. Any construction of it that we make can only be theoretical and will not correspond with the amphictyony as it existed at any point in time; we have also to reckon with the inevitable gulf between theory and practice. The data which serve to confirm the model to some extent are scattered and indirect, and can only properly be evaluated by scholars. Details can, however, be added from more specialist modern studies, and a reading of Judges 4 and 5 with a modern commentary will be a useful introduction.

We shall have to move further back now, from the traditions of the Yahwist to the traditions of the amphictyony. The explanation of its origin is that the tribes which make it up are twelve brothers, descended from a single father, Israel (Jacob) and a variety of mothers. It is surely not unreasonable to think that this is too good to be true. Not that we are to rule out links of kinship between the tribes, but artificial genealogies are too much a part of the tradition of ancient communities to be accepted without question.

In accord with this tradition of kinship, the tribes are said to have entered Palestine to take up their allotted territories in a concerted invasion. But here, too, we must be careful. The problems of unity and liaison between the tribal amphictyony in its later stages, and the limited amount of the country which it had managed to occupy, suggest that other explanations must be considered.

In addition to the mainstream of the Old Testament narrative we have two additional sources of information to make use of. Within the Old Testament itself, we can collect information from genealogies, tribal lists, poetry, fragmentary records put in another context, and incidental references from unrelated material. Outside the Old Testament we can make use of archaeological evidence. Not, however, as simple corroboration. That is a questionable process. A rather more reliable method is possible. By and large there is enough material from Egyptian records and elsewhere which, together with archaeology, can offer the beginnings of a description of the way in which the occupation of Palestine changed over the time of the Israelite settlement, so that we have a background on which to put what we discover from the Old Testament itself. As this is a complex process, a more detailed quotation will be helpful to indicate what is involved.

It is obvious that in a country where men have dwelt for a long time, settlement by invading tribes will not only have a powerful effect on the way of life of both the former inhabitants and the newcomers, but will also have a substantial effect on the country itself. Now the circumstances of people's lives are easily liable to change: this would be the first effect of the settlement, and when they had been thrown into confusion they would only gradually be brought back to stability. That is why it is necessary to examine very carefully the other much more constant factor, which forms a background that it is difficult to alter. Besides examining the history of the tribes and people, it is possible to investigate the history of a country's territorial divisions in complete independence of other aspects of the problem; and this we must do if we are to gain a clear understanding of the settlement, the conditions preceding it, and its effects. . . .

Throughout history territorial divisions, ultimately dependent on the lie of the land, are extremely persistent; even changes of population hardly ever overthrow them completely, but bring about, at most, minor alterations. In studying their development, then, it is always best to cover as long a period as possible. . . . Only when we have ascertained the state of the territorial divisions that were developed and established before the Israelites appeared, and worked back from the forms they took in the period that followed, in order to find out what remained of the old divisions and what was altered, can we make a true estimate of the effect of the settlement on the political geography of the country. But it no longer matters very much whether the tradition provides us with direct evidence of the details of the settlement; even if there were no evidence at all, it would be possible by comparing the territorial divisions before and after the settlement to say for certain what happened in the obscure period between.[4]

This is an ambitious programme – some might say far too ambitious – but the fact remains that it has been carried out with fair success; and after it has been carried through in practice, an important conclusion is reached which in essentials (though details have been changed slightly since it was first expressed over forty years ago) still holds and fits in with what we saw of the amphictyony in the time of Saul. The Israelite occupation of Palestine was

the occupation of those parts of the country which already formed large political units, and continued to do so afterwards, i.e., principally the mountains, which had been only slightly affected by the spread of the city-state system. These territories, as yet ill-organized politically, and probably still thinly populated, were least capable of resisting the advance of the Israelites, and offered them the best opportunity of settling down and gradually turning from their semi-nomadic way of life to an agricultural economy. In contrast to this, the city-state system established in the plains at first encountered the Israelite occupation only at its outlying points; and only a small part of it was destroyed immediately.[5]

Against this roughly-sketched background we can now turn to the Old Testament itself.

If we look at the names of the tribes which go to make up the league, we find that while twelve are usually listed, the names of the tribes tend to differ. As with the twelve apostles, it is difficult to reach an agreed list. Genesis 49, which may be quite old, lists twelve sons of Jacob: Reuben, Simeon, Levi, Judah, Zebulun, Issachar, Dan, Gad, Asher, Naphthali, Joseph and Benjamin. Deuteronomy 33, the 'Blessing of Moses', omits Simeon and to compensate divides the house of Joseph into two sons, Ephraim and Manasseh. Numbers 26.5–51 includes Simeon, but this time leaves out Levi.[6]

There are further complications. When the tribal boundaries are listed, very little territory is allotted to Reuben, though he is the firstborn. Simeon, too, has an ambiguous position and is fitted into part of the territory of Judah. Levi has no territory at all. The Song of Deborah (Judges 5), mentioned above, lists Machir and Gilead on the same level as the tribes. All this suggests that the tribal lists reflect various stages of the twelve-tribe structure. Levi is very much a mystery: in later history, of course, the Levites were a priestly clan, but Genesis 34 shows Levi in warlike action with Simeon. Reuben and Simeon seem once to have been important, but at a later stage to have suffered a decline.[7]

One further feature is sometimes noted. Some of the

tribes seem to bear names which they could have acquired only after they had settled in Palestine: Judah, Ephraim and Naphthali are probably place-names rather than personal names; Benjamin may well mean 'living in the south', and Issachar means 'labourer'. We may even have to take into account the added complication that the settlement did not just consist in the *movement* of tribes, but led to the *formation* of tribes in particular areas over a space of time.[8]

At this point a glance at Judges 1 will be illuminating. Here we have a general picture of the settlement which bears out much of what has just been said; the tribes have some difficulty in making headway, particularly against the fortified cities in the plain, and some even become subject to Canaanite rule. The settlement seems to be a piecemeal move taking place in various different areas, rather than one concerted attempt.

The way to go on from here would be to try to construct a history of each individual tribe and its movements, but that is impossible now;[9] we shall have to look at the situation in more general terms. We have to go on to ask what this 'settlement' was, and by whom it was made.

According to the main Old Testament narrative the settlement was a conquest by a group which had invaded Palestine after their miraculous deliverance from Egypt. And there is no reason for us to doubt that basically this was the history of some of the settlers in Palestine. In view of the fragmentary form of the settlement, however, we cannot conclude that *all* the tribes were in some way involved; at the very least, a more thorough study would show that some 'tribal' activity was going on in Palestine during the times when the 'Israelites' were still in Egypt. Later tradition, of course, attributes the Exodus and the covenant at Mount Sinai to all Israel, but there are parallels to the memories of a group being taken over by a larger whole: a more modern confederation, the United States of America, for example, has as 'American' memories events in which only a small part of the present Union was involved.[10]

We shall be tracing the core of the tribal alliance further back in a moment; meanwhile we have to see how it was associated with the varied movements that were taking place throughout Palestine.

Canaan at this period was involved in a widespread social rebellion. Diplomatic correspondence dating from the fourteenth century BC, discovered at Tell el-Amarna in Egypt, on the site of the city of the Pharaoh Akhenaten, shows Egyptian rule of Palestine breaking up under pressure from the Ḥabiru. When these letters were first discovered, over-hasty identification of the Ḥabiru with the Hebrews was attempted, but the answer is not as easy as that (in any case, this period is still too early for the settlement, which took place over a century and a half later). Ḥabiru were soon discovered elsewhere in the Near East, among the Hittites, in Mari on the Middle Euphrates and Nuzi east of the Tigris, and in Egypt. They seem to have been members of a social group widespread over the Near East, sometimes (in Syria and Palestine) appearing as marauders, but in Egypt as foreign labourers. It is therefore impossible that all Ḥabiru were Hebrews. On the other hand, there is no conclusive reason why some at least of the Israelites were not Ḥabiru, just one part of the movement.[11]

As no more than a working hypothesis, then, it is possible that the 'settlement' is a development in the revolution in which the Ḥabiru were involved. In Palestine there was a break-up of the feudal system brought about by a kind of peasant's revolt; those involved sought an alternative system to that of the Canaanite chain of city-states which had oppressed them beyond tolerance. Added impetus and a specific direction were provided by the sizable group coming in from Egypt with their distinctive beliefs. Such a theory would certainly explain the fragmentariness of the settlement; the fact of the original diversity would explain the difficulty which the amphictyony seems to have had in keeping together (the tendency to become too closely assimilated to the social life of the environment, in tension with the demands of the faith of the core of the alliance); the theory would also explain the vivid hatred of the Canaanites which can be found right through the Old Testament and is perhaps surprising if explained simply as an

67

attitude communicated by a relatively limited group of invaders.[12]

Now all this has represented the settlement as being dominantly peaceful. What about the warlike account to be found in Joshua 1–12 in which cities are destroyed with fire and sword? And is there not archaeological evidence in support of such destruction?

There is, but it is difficult to use. In the 1930s it was thought that conclusive evidence had been found to support the tradition of the destruction of Jericho by the Israelites; later investigations in the 1950s, however, told a different story. The destruction had taken place much earlier than had previously been supposed, and by the time the Israelites are held to have appeared on the scene there would have been nothing but a ruin.[13] But that is only half the matter. Thorough excavations at Hazor, a large city in upper Galilee, carried on in the late 1950s, seem to support the account of its destruction in Joshua 11, at the time recorded.[14]

In fact, there is no reason why a certain amount of destruction of this kind should not have accompanied a general movement of the type we have just seen, particularly in outlying areas. What is more doubtful is whether we should see it as part of a concerted campaign. Furthermore, leaving aside the difficulties of the Joshua account (and there are many), if we study it carefully we shall see that in essentials it is even in its present form limited to quite a small area. It is essentially a Benjaminite tradition, describing a campaign in central Palestine in highly theological terms. Only in its present context has it been generalized.[15]

Now associated with this is a nice point. If this is – as it seems to be – essentially Benjaminite tradition, what is Joshua, an Ephraimite, doing here as a leader? Here we have another of the problems which harass scholars. It is not unusual for traditions to cluster round prominent figures – this can certainly be seen in the case of Moses, and the story of Goliath may have been transferred to David from elsewhere – and that has probably happened here. Joshua seems to belong firmly in the tradition at the end of Joshua (ch. 24) in the territory of Shechem, where a covenant ceremony is held. He was probably instrumental in uniting the merging groups of tribes and was associated with other events at a later date.[16]

The main impulse towards the integration would come from the incoming group of tribes, and it is to them that we must now turn. Here, too, we must reckon with the possibility of further fragmentation of the tradition, but in this case it has probably been exaggerated.

Struck by some summary passages which make no mention of the events on Mount Sinai, some scholars have concluded that the tradition of the law-giving there was originally separate from that of the Exodus. The groups assembling on Mount Sinai were not those which had come out of Egypt. A reasonable argument can be made out for this conclusion, but it is far from being decisive. Whatever happened at Sinai, the oldest collections of traditions make it an integral part of the complex of events which make up the deliverance of the Israelites from Egypt; to separate the two presents a mass of difficulties.[17]

But that is not to say that there has not been later addition and reinterpretation. On the contrary, just as we come to the central events of the Old Testament, the events which seem to have brought belief in Yahweh to birth and to have shaped the life of Israel, the difficulties become thicker than ever. Just what happened on Sinai? What was the Exodus? The answer is not far short of being 'we do not really know'.

These two events, rather than having been remembered particularly clearly in historical terms, have been a point of constant reinterpretation of all kinds. Thus it is impossible to separate the story of the Exodus from the tradition of the institution of the Passover, which is in fact a pastoral festival with very different roots; and whatever did happen on Sinai (or Horeb, and there can be no certainty as to exactly where that was), the original event has been overlaid by later ideas and later legislation. It was the custom of Israel to attribute all its laws to Moses, whether historically they went back to his time or not, and cultic influence will have been at work here, too. Careful investigation may discover some of the stages by which the narrative complexes grew, enabling us to penetrate a little further towards the original events; any detailed knowledge of them, however, seems to be lost, perhaps for ever.

In addition to wide-scale reinterpretation, there is a further complication which holds not only at this point, but elsewhere in the Old Testament. This is the tendency of the Israelites, like other peoples, to project into the past explanations of present customs or sacred objects or even landmarks. In this case, a story can look like a tradition of a past event but will in fact be the opposite; it will be wholly constructed backwards from the present. To take an example: Numbers 21 contains a story of how God sent fiery serpents among the Israelites, so that many of them were killed. Moses was commanded to make a bronze serpent and set it on a pole; if any one was bitten, he would look at the serpent and live. The story is isolated, without any close connection with its present context, and can clearly be treated on its own. Scholars note that this is the only time that a bronze serpent appears in the narrative of the journey to Palestine – unlike, say, the ark or tabernacle, both of which appear time and again. There is, however, evidence of there having been a bronze serpent in the Jerusalem temple at one time. We may therefore imagine that it was taken over with the temple at David's peaceful occupation of Jerusalem. Like other Canaanite features, it was baptized into Israelite faith, in this case by being associated with Moses in the creative period of the Israelite past. There are probably a great many other examples, particularly in Genesis, Joshua and Judges. Lot's wife is doubtless a story attached to a remarkable physical feature; in Judges 4.5 we have a 'palm of Deborah' associated with the wrong Deborah (another danger!) and the story of Ai (Joshua 8) is probably also a narrative of this nature. The technical term is 'aetiology'. More complex developments lie behind the famous story of the golden calf, but it is probably essentially of the same kind.

As if this were not enough, there is, as we saw briefly with Joshua, the tendency to transfer stories from elsewhere to distinguished figures in the tradition; this has certainly happened with Moses. Moses was not the first baby of whom it is related that he was found in the bulrushes.

Nevertheless, the attempt must be made to say something more positive about these central events, however tentatively. Here, after all, is the point from which the people o-Israel traced their special character as a chosen people. Furthermore, the deliverance from Egypt and the covenant with Yahweh were not only reinterpreted time and again in Israelite faith, but also taken up into Christianity as the imagery best fitted to express the meaning of the death and resurrection of Jesus. As will immediately become clear, for the most part we shall have to confess ignorance. Historically, this is, of course, frustrating; but as we shall see in the last chapter, this ignorance is not perhaps as damaging as it might seem.

It was the Yahwist's view that Yahweh had been God from the beginning of the world and that worship of him had first been instituted by Enoch (Genesis 4.26). This, however, will be a theological rather than a historical judgment. The other traditions in the Pentateuch, and numerous references in the prophetic books (see especially Hosea 11.1; 13.4ff.; Jeremiah 2) agree that Israel first worshipped Yahweh in the desert after leaving Egypt. Thus Moses would seem to have been principally involved in bringing knowledge of Yahweh to the people (Exodus 3.14). What the name Yahweh means and where it comes from we do not know; scholars can only offer guesses: some have read profound meanings into the famous explanation 'I am who I am' (*ehyeh 'asher ehyeh*); others have seen this as no more than a riddle-like phrase hinting at the name Yahweh. He is repeatedly associated with Sinai, even described as 'Lord of Sinai', but how and by whom he may have been worshipped before Moses is again completely obscure.[18]

According to the tradition, Moses, having fled from Egypt, experienced a call from Yahweh to lead the Hebrew groups captive in Egypt out of the country. After their escape, they came to Sinai and made a covenant with Yahweh who had delivered them. The sequence is most important. It is sometimes argued that Israelite belief arose out of the experience of the Hebrews coming out of Egypt through subsequent interpretation of miraculous, or apparently miraculous, events which happened to them *en route*. Looking back on these events, the Hebrews believed that they represented the hand of God. Such a view, however, is a modern rationalization which is very difficult to support from the actual tradition. According to the tradition, the Exodus and Sinai narratives are not later interpretations attaching significance to the historical events; these events were announced before they took place.

> Far from representing the divine acts as the basis of all knowledge of God and all communication with him, [the texts] represent God as communicating freely with men, and particularly with Moses, before, during and after these events. Far from the incident at the burning bush being an 'interpretation' of the divine acts, it is a direct communication from God to Moses of his purposes and intentions. This conversation, instead of being represented as an interpretation of the divine act, is a precondition of it. If God had not told Moses what he did, the Israelites would not have demanded their escape from Egypt and the deliverance at the Sea of Reeds would not have taken place.[19]

Our own 'reinterpretation', then, can be slanted in a wrong direction. The point is only made in passing, but it is important that it should be made, as it will appear again in connection with the prophets, and occupy us briefly in the final chapter.[20]

The images used to describe Yahweh give some indication of the way in which he was pictured; another reading of the Song of Deborah will illustrate this more than any list of epithets, and the experiences of Yahweh described in the rest of Judges and in I Samuel will bear it out. Yahweh is a God of force, of power, of holiness. Whether he is the only God is not a question which is raised at this period; but his characteristics make him the only God for those who worship him.

All this is reflected in the laws which mark the people's response to Yahweh. Difficult though it is to detect the earliest strata below the level of the later additions, the character of exclusiveness which marks off the people of

Yahweh from their neighbours is a counterpart to the characteristics of their God. Moses is involved here, too, but it is again difficult to assess his work exactly.

The action of Yahweh and the people's response are bound up in the form of the covenant, a pattern of alliance of which there are examples elsewhere in the Near East. What the original form of the covenant was, and when the pattern as now presented in the Old Testament first emerged, is difficult to discover because of the inevitable later interpretation; at a later stage other groups were included in the covenant, some notably at Shechem, where a god of the Covenant (El Berith) was worshipped (a ceremony of this kind is described in Joshua 24). This may have influenced the form of the covenant. But whatever its origin, the covenant became a focal point in Israelite belief. In the covenant, the God who had delivered his people bound himself to them, and in return demanded their allegiance.[21]

One final step back remains. Before the account of the Exodus and settlement, the Old Testament has the stories of the patriarchs, Abraham, Isaac and Jacob. We have already seen that it is improbable that they worshipped Yahweh, and so far they have played no part in our picture. Who were they, and where do they belong?

From the tradition, we have a picture of them as 'semi-nomads', living in tents and keeping livestock, moving on to new land after a while. Archaeologists see them as part of an Aramaean migration early in the second millennium BC, and parallels to several features in the stories can be traced from neighbouring cultures of the time. Of course, the stories have been very considerably rewritten, above all that of Joseph, which comprises most of Genesis 37 to 48. Here we shall be able to recognize a very close relation of the Succession Narrative, the story of the success of a wise man which is almost too good to be true. Nor will this be the only part where later hands have been at work.

Much, again, is past rediscovering, but there are some hints which can be developed further. First, the patriarchs move in particular areas: Abraham is largely associated with the south, and Jacob with the north-east. As the tradition now stands, the figure of Isaac is a shadowy one, with hardly any significance in his own right. (The traditions attached to Abraham and Jacob may well be more complex than they appear; the variant spellings of Abraham and Abram might represent different figures, and the Abraham of Genesis 14 has long been seen to have a different character from the rest of the saga. The dual name Jacob/Israel is also a probable sign that two traditions have been amalgamated – we are much too early for the Saul/Paul type conjunction!) The patriarchs are also associated with particular sanctuaries at which the god El is worshipped: we find a god El 'Elyon at Jerusalem (Gen. 14.17ff.), El 'Olam at Beersheba (Gen. 21.33), El Bethel at Bethel (Gen. 31.13), El Shaddai, who may originally have been associated with Mamre (Gen. 18.1), El Roi at Beer-lahai-roi (Gen. 16.13f.), and even an El-Elohe-Israel at Shechem (Gen. 33.20). These are not separate gods, but a series of local manifestations of the Canaanite high god El (as a parallel to the one god and his many manifestations one could compare the different cults of Jupiter and Venus; even, perhaps, in a different way the various manifestations of the Virgin). El was the head of the pantheon of Canaanite gods and was regarded as a wise father figure, as well as creator god.[22]

Now the shrines to El were almost certainly not founded by the patriarchs; these cults go back beyond their time, and the stories linking the patriarchs with the El shrines are probably to be seen as aetiologies, of the kind we discussed earlier, associating the patriarchs with the shrines. At the same time, we can also trace a second pattern of religion within the stories: each patriarch is associated with a particular clan god in a personal relationship. So we have the Shield of Abraham (Gen. 15.1), the Kinsman of Isaac (Gen. 31.42) and the Mighty One of Jacob (49.24). In the tradition as we have it, of course, these names have been run together and regarded as titles of Yahweh, but a passage like Genesis 31.36–54 shows how we are in fact dealing with different figures. These gods are not associated with particular places but with particular groups, to whom they were bound in a kind of personal relationship.

Both these elements seem to be important ingredients in later Israelite belief. The worship of El, in particular, seems to have brought an important new dimension into belief in Yahweh. Between El and Yahweh there was never the antipathy that there was between Yahweh and Baal, and some of the characteristics of El seem to have gradually been transferred to Yahweh. At the least, it is important to note the name which the tribal alliance bore – Israel: El will strive. Much, however, also remains obscure, not least the further details of the patriarchs themselves. Features which have already been noted, and others which there is not space to enumerate, make it virtually certain that the kinship between Abraham, Isaac and Jacob is a later construction, bringing hitherto unrelated figures into an artificial relationship. Over a distance of almost four thousand years it is amazing that we can discover as much as we have.

And so we come to the furthest point we can reach. There have been many complications – perhaps, it may seem, too many – and we may seem to have departed a long way from the biblical tradition. Yet all these questions are raised by the tradition, and if the account seems complicated, one thing is quite certain: it has without doubt erred on the side of not being complicated enough.

We ended the previous chapter and began this with some reflections on the work of the Yahwist(s); some further reflections will serve as a transition back to that time, and to the move forward that we must now make:

That they imposed unity upon their material is evident; they produced a reasonably smooth narrative of the encounter of Yahweh with Israel which has still not been analysed into its components. The historian is inclined to say that they imposed a false unity upon the material; but the historian is a stranger to the wisdom approach to reality. All of these traditions had met in historic Israel, the people of Yahweh, and each item was an episode in the recital of the acts of Yahweh. The kinship of Abraham and Jacob may be a fictitious construction of the sages, but the union of the groups who recognized these men as their ancestors was a historical reality, a reality of experience. Who was involved in the Egypt and Sinai experiences we do not know and probably shall never know. Neither, it seems, did the sages, but they were convinced that the union of all those who worshipped Yahweh had not happened by chance, and it should not be narrated as if it had happened by chance. It is again the principle of experience; the scribes could answer their questions only by reflection upon the narrated experience of the groups which formed Israel.[23]

Attention is drawn here to the unity of Israel. In the view of the Yahwist this might be plain, but as we turn now to the events and features of the monarchy we shall see that unity was far from being achieved.

NOTES

1. For more details see John Bright, *A History of Israel* (London and Philadelphia, 1960), pp. 128 ff.; M. Noth, *The History of Israel* (London and New York, 1960²), pp. 85 ff.

2. For more detail see *The Oxford Classical Dictionary*, p. 44.

3. See T. C. Vriezen, *The Religion of Ancient Israel* (London and Philadelphia, 1967), pp. 163 ff.

4. See A. Alt, 'The Settlement of the Israelites in Palestine', in: *Essays in Old Testament History and Religion* (Oxford, 1966), p. 136.

5. Alt, p. 168.

6. Noth, *History of Israel*, p. 85; J. L. McKenzie, *The World of the Judges* (New Jersey and London, 1967), p. 81.

7. For further details see the books by Bright, Noth and McKenzie.

8. Noth, *History of Israel*, pp. 53 ff.

9. An attempt is made by Noth in the passage mentioned in the previous note.

10. McKenzie, *The World of the Judges*, p. 109.

11. See F. F. Bruce, 'Tell el-Amarna', in: *Archaeology and Old Testament Study*, pp. 3 ff.; also M. Weippert, *Die Landnahme der Israelitischen Stämme* (Göttingen, 1967), pp. 66 f. (An English translation is in preparation under the title *The Settlement of the Israelite Tribes in Palestine*.)

12. For further details see *The World of the Judges*, pp. 76 ff. A variant of this theory was first put forward by G. E. Mendenhall, *Law and Covenant in Ancient Israel* (Pittsburgh, 1955), and is criticized by Weippert, pp. 59 ff. The version by McKenzie followed here seems less open to these criticisms.

13. See Kathleen Kenyon, 'Jericho', in: *Archaeology and Old Testament Study*, pp. 264 ff.

14. See Y. Yadin, 'Hazor', in *Archaeology and Old Testament Study*, pp. 245 ff.

15. For details, see *The World of the Judges*, pp. 45 ff.; M. Noth, *Das Buch Josua* (Tübingen, 1953), pp. 20 ff.

16. *The World of the Judges*, pp. 98 ff.

17. For a popular account which does not find the difficulties insuperable, see J. H. Otwell, *A New Approach to the Old Testament* (Nashville and London, 1968).

18. For more details, see T. C. Vriezen, *The Religion of Ancient Israel*, pp. 124 ff.

19. James Barr, 'Revelation in the Old Testament and in Theology' in Martin E. Marty and Dean Peerman (eds.), *New Theology* 1 (New York, 1963), p. 65. The whole article is particularly important. See, too, his *Old and New in Interpretation* (London and New York, 1966), pp. 65 ff.

20. See pp. 91, 119.

21. For more details of the covenant and its forms see E. W. Nicholson, *Deuteronomy and Tradition* (Oxford, 1967), pp. 43f.; Bright, *History of Israel*, pp. 136f.

22. See Vriezen, *The Religion of Ancient Israel*, pp. 102ff.; R. E. Clements, *God and Temple* (Oxford, 1965), pp. 9ff.

23. J. L. McKenzie, 'Reflections on Wisdom', p. 7.

5 Problems of the Present

The picture of events leading up to the reign of David has been one of diverse elements needing to be brought together into a unity, both politically and theologically, and we have seen how unity was sought by David, on the one hand, and the Yahwist (and his successors), on the other. We should, however, be careful not to exaggerate the historical reality of the unity or the area over which it was achieved. When using traditions which see the past so very much in the light of the present, this is a recurrent temptation, just as this same perspective also tends to over-emphasize the degree to which the people of any one age were clear about the right way forward. The division between 'orthodox' and 'heretic' in a time of enquiring is one that is drawn after the event, and so, too, to some degree will have been the distinction between what was the religion of Israel and what was not. Palestine is a country with extremely varied terrain and areas of poor communication; we also know how long it takes for ideas and patterns of life to extend their influence, and so the spectrum of Israelite[1] religion will have been very wide indeed. What we know of it now can only be a selected part. Inevitably, in all this variety, there was a good deal of scope for conflict.

In looking at the wise men, we saw that they were part of a change in the political system which also had religious significance. The same thing is true to an even greater degree in the case of the king. Just what the religious significance of the king could be will be seen from brief descriptions of his status in the two neighbouring countries to Israel, Egypt and Mesopotamia. In Egypt:

Pharaoh, the king, is himself a real god, in whom all divinity is incarnated. This is manifest even in art, where Pharaoh is always represented in superhuman proportions as the only person who acts, makes war, storms fortresses, slays the enemy, offers sacrifice, and so on. He is the equal of the gods, and himself an object of worship. Officially he is called 'the good god'. His title, 'Lord of the two lands', implies that he rules over the entire dualistic universe. In himself he embodies and holds in harmonious equilibrium the powers, Life and Death, the gods Horus and Seth, who are in conflict, and yet, by the very tension between them, create and renew life.[2]

In Mesopotamia the king has rather a different status, but it is viewed in not dissimilar terms. There:

Kingship was a sacral institution; and the king shared the holiness of the institution to such an extent that we are justified in speaking of his divinity. In so far as the king is endowed with divine powers and qualities he may be regarded as a divine being; but he is not a god in the same sense as Pharaoh. . . . In accordance with the will of the god he administers and governs the whole land, which is really the god's property, or the world and mankind, whom the gods created for their own service. . . . The king is the intermediary between gods and men, but he also represents the people before the gods and is responsible for relations between them.[3]

Less is known about kingship in Canaan, in Israel's immediate environment, but it is thought to have followed the pattern of kingship in Mesopotamia.[4]

Saul, of course, was little more than a chieftain and was not involved in a period of change. In the case of David, however, in his new capital at Jerusalem and with a position parallel to the rulers of neighbouring empires, associations of this kind cannot have been far away. Nevertheless, David shows signs of considerable care in his work of unification and it is instructive to see how carefully he moved.

The ancient Jebusite city of Jerusalem itself needed to be integrated with the earlier structure of the tribal alliance, and to do this David had the ark, the former focal point of the amphictyony, transferred to Jerusalem with ceremony and given a prominent place there (II Sam. 6). The city from which the king ruled was thus at the same time to be the place to which the tribes would naturally look. It did not immediately receive pre-eminence, for in Solomon's time the 'great high place' was still Gibeon, where Solomon himself sacrificed, to the disapproval of a later editor. In due course, however, it occupied pride of place, after the building of Solomon's temple there, so that when the northern part of the kingdom broke away its king felt it necessary to set up rival places of worship at Dan and Bethel (I Kings 12.26 ff.). But what was the relationship between the king and the beliefs of the tribes, and what was his place in the new scheme of things?

A look at II Sam. 7 and Psalm 132 (though the former has been developed by later editors) will show the solution that was reached. A covenant, a new covenant, bound Yahweh to David and to Zion (Jerusalem). He had chosen Jerusalem and he had chosen David and his descendants to be kings there. The Davidic covenant differed strongly in type from that associated with Sinai. The Sinai covenant, as we have seen, was one in which Israel undertook to follow certain laws in response to the action of Yahweh as a condition of the continuation of the covenant. The covenant with David, on the other hand, was one of promise, accompanied by the assertion that the covenant would last for ever. The question of conditions under which the covenant would not continue is not raised. How this covenant arose is not at all clear.[5] It runs parallel to a tradition of an earlier covenant of a similar kind with Abraham as described in Genesis 15, but we cannot suppose that it arose directly out of this earlier covenant. After what we have seen, we must allow for at least the mutual influence of one on the other. One suggestion is that

the royal covenant of II Sam. 7 was influenced in its origin by other near Eastern conceptions of kingship, especially that which was current in the Canaanite city states. It is a false contrast to set Israel's idea of the divine election of its kings too sharply against the elaborate court style of the ancient Near East, since the idea of the divine election of kings was current in the ancient world, and the dynastic covenant of II Sam. 7 shows us the distinctive form which this belief in royal election took in Israel.[6]

Whatever the background, though, the Davidic covenant certainly served as a useful piece of political theology.

There is a strong tradition that David did not build a temple, though he may well have had associations with the royal temple which would have existed from pre-Israelite Jerusalem. The reason given by later tradition is that his hands were soiled from war (I Chron. 22.8); it is equally likely that he did not want to move forward too quickly and jeopardize the unity of his empire. The reign of Solomon, however, did see a new development in this direction. A new temple was built, and built not by Israelites but by craftsmen specially brought in from Phoenicia for the purpose (a temple approximating to the design of the Jerusalem temple has in fact been found in recent archaeological work in Phoenicia). Israel thus had a royal state temple, and in this way came that much nearer to the pattern of life of its neighbours.

I Kings gives us a description of the temple and all its furnishings. Some things may have been altered in the description, and the factors governing the tradition mentioned earlier must not be forgotten. Despite the central place accorded to the temple, remarkably little is said in the Old Testament about what actually went on there – so much so that immense scope has been left for scholars' conjectures. We have three ways of filling in the picture and the king's place in it more fully: from the descriptions of the temple itself, from comparisons with neighbouring cultures, and from the book of Psalms.

The temple and its furnishings were full of cosmic symbolism – like other Near Eastern temples it was meant as a symbol of its god's abode. The bronze sea, the supporting oxen, the altar of burnt offering and the decoration within the temple all point to the cosmos and especially to the fertility of the earth. A strong argument can even be made out for the association of temple worship with the sun; among other things, the temple seems to have been oriented so that the sun rising over the Mount of Olives at the autumn equinox shone directly into the Holy of Holies.[7] All this shows influence from surrounding cultures.

Now, of course, it can be argued that this is a matter of externals, and is to be attributed to the foreign builders

81

building a temple the only way they knew how, or that whereas Israel took over the *form* of the worship of her neighbours, the *content* was changed. But these arguments are dubious ones. It is extremely doubtful how far we can separate form and content in rites of worship, and it is also doubtful how far in the pre-exilic period worship in Jerusalem lived up to the standards set by contemporary and later Yahwism. We are up against the problem of exactly what Israelite religion was in practice, and here – at different periods, at any rate – there often seems to have been a great gap between what was done and what should have been done. Hence the prophets' polemic and stricter injunctions in later codes of law. We find constant reforms attempted by Israelite kings; we find human sacrifice and sacred prostitution and altars to other gods, and:

> What are we to say when we find in the record the gardens of Adonis, Ezekiel's chambers of imagery, women weeping for Tammuz, women declaring that since they ceased baking cakes for the Queen of Heaven nothing has gone well with them, the *maṣṣeboth*, the asherahs, the divinations, the 'seeking unto the *elohim*', and numerous other practices?[8]

This shows what the spiritual climate of the country could be.

The reason for introducing this picture of deviation to be found in the record is so that we are warned against making too 'orthodox' and stereotyped a model of Israelite worship, and so that we have it at the back of our mind when considering the relationship between Israel and elsewhere. In fact we constantly come upon traces of a long battle between Yahwism and the luxuriant religion of the country which the tribal alliance was making its own, a battle in which the Yahwist view was not always on the winning side.

All this makes comparisons with neighbouring countries so difficult. Where we have to use analogy to fill in the picture, just what alterations do we have to allow for? Just how far did ideas and worship change in the Israelite context? It is desperately difficult to judge, and as a result we have here an area where various schools of scholars conflict. At best, a two-way procedure, interpreting the

Psalms with other Near Eastern practices in view and then revising points in the analogies in the light of the Psalms, can be adopted, and then as always the obscurities remain.

Nevertheless, the Psalms can tell us a good deal. Those we have in the Psalter have sometimes been rewritten and revised, and a number may date in their entirety from after the exile. But there is every reason to suppose that we have much material reaching back to the early days of the monarchy, and perhaps even to David himself, to whom the Psalter is attributed. There are drawbacks; psalms are by nature general and their information is rarely about specific occasions. Even reconstructing ritual actions, let alone festivals, from them is hard. There is, however, valuable light to be had.[9]

In the Psalms, Jerusalem itself takes on a new appearance. Psalms 48 and 46 respectively transfer to it the attributes of the mountain in the north, where the Canaanite god Baal was believed to dwell, and of the mythological river of paradise which watered God's dwelling place (see, too, what has been said above about the temple).[10] From a group of royal psalms, e.g. Psalms 2, 21, 45, 72, 110, in addition to Psalm 132, at which we have already looked, we can see features of the king which are similar to those to be found elsewhere in the Near East and support for these features can be found in passing references in other Old Testament passages.[11] His birth can be described in pictures taken from the birth of a god; through being anointed he is filled with power and wisdom. He is servant of Yahweh in a different sense from anyone else and can be called his son; and as son of Yahweh, the God of all the earth, he has a rightful claim to world-wide dominion. Without him, the people perish; under him, they see prosperity:

> The king is the saviour to whom the people look for salvation, both in the negative sense of deliverance from enemies, danger and need, and in the widest positive sense of good fortune and well-being. It is his duty to provide this. This is the picture which the royal psalms give of the king and his 'righteousness'.[12]

In other countries, this reverence for the king and concern for fertility and prosperity found a climax in a great annual festival, held either in the spring or in the autumn, to celebrate the might of their god and ensure the well-being of the land for another year. In this festival the king, with his special relationship with the god, played a central part. As usual, the evidence for the existence of such a feast in Jerusalem and for the details, if it was indeed celebrated, is difficult to assess, but there are numerous passages which seem to fit best on the hypothesis of such a festival.

A list of elements which could occur in a New Year festival of this kind was given over a generation ago as follows:

(a) The dramatic representation of the death and resurrection of the god.
(b) The recitation or symbolic representation of the myth of creation.
(c) The ritual combat, in which the triumph of the god over his enemies was depicted.
(d) The sacred marriage (between the king and his chosen consort).
(e) The triumphal procession, in which the king played the part of the god followed by a train of lesser gods or visiting deities.[13]

Although it was put forward tentatively and with qualifications, it has been subjected to a great deal of criticism by later scholars, who challenged the presence of some of the elements in particular cultures and almost all of them in Israel. They protested that Yahweh was not a god like this; that there was no real evidence; that Israel was very different. But we have already seen the lengths to which religious practices in Israel seem to have gone at times, and in view of the nature of what evidence we have there is little room for dogmatism either way.

There are passages in the Psalms, perhaps to be supplemented by elements in the 'Servant Songs' in the book of Isaiah, which can be interpreted in the context of a ritual according to which at least the king has undergone symbolical death for a night, to return to life in the morning;[14] Psalms like 74 and 89 contain elements of the myth of creation, and we have already seen the symbolic representations of the cosmos which were to be found in the temple; Psalm 89 also, like Psalms 2 and 18, points to some kind of ritual combat.[15] It has been argued that II Sam. 6 culminates in a sacred marriage and that this is the background to the enigmatic words that David exchanges with Michal there;[16] whether or not this is so,

> the second chapter of Hosea, to take only one example, shows that there were levels of religion in Israel, widely spread throughout the country, in which Yahweh was spoken of as a Baal and was associated in popular thought with those sexual elements in the fertility cults of Canaan whose existence is well attested. If this is denied, Hosea's polemic loses its point and the poignancy of his transformation of the ritual marriage element in that level of Israelite religion which he is attacking into the magnificent symbolism of the spiritual marriage between Yahweh and a repentant Israel is destroyed.[17]

A triumphal procession is easier to point to: from the procession which brought the ark to Jerusalem onwards, we have indications of processions, not least in the magnificent Psalms 24 and 68.[18]

The subject is so complex, and the evidence so difficult to interpret, that this brief discussion can be no more than a hint of the rich variety of myth and ritual associated with the temple and the king. To those unfamiliar with patterns of this kind, it is an element that perhaps needs to be stressed in case – to say it once again – we are tempted to interpret Israelite worship too narrowly. On the other hand, the points which have been brought out must not let us forget that this was after all *Israelite* religion. In this complex there must be found room also for the covenants with David and Israel which bound Yahweh to them and for the ark, the sacred object of the tribal alliance: it is one of the weaknesses of modern scholarship that the different approaches adopted tend to lay excessive emphasis either on the more exotic elements at which we have been looking, to the exclusion of these, or to the narrowly Israelite elements, at the risk of ignoring features which must certainly be taken into account. Before we see the picture more fully, it will be essential for scholars to attempt to reconcile these different stresses more closely.[19]

One trouble is that this picture of king and temple has to be drawn very much in the flat. Our sources give us no indication at all of how the ideology of kingship and temple developed over the almost four hundred years between Solomon and the fall of Jerusalem. Over a period of this kind changes must have taken place, but we know nothing about them. That is the measure of our ignorance, which must make even the fullest account fall far short of a history.

One thing, however, we do know; that after the death of Solomon the northern kingdom broke away from the south and until its destruction in 721 BC had a different succession of kings from that in the south. The reasons for this breakaway are complex and will have been a mixture of religious and political motives: the north consisted of ten of the ancient tribes and so the original policy may have been intended as a return to an earlier pattern. But if this was so, it did not succeed: in his promotion of two northern shrines to rival Jerusalem, Jeroboam placed in them the image of a bull – an ancient symbol which may even have links with patriarchal times, but one nevertheless which led the way to excessive assimilation between the worship of Yahweh and the worship of Baal. From then on we hear nothing but condemnation of the north.[20]

We have, however, to remember that our sources are southern ones and that they probably do the situation less than justice. Excess there may have been, but there was undoubtedly preservation of old patterns; at least one reform programme which we shall look at later began its life in the north. Furthermore, to avoid odious comparisons, and to make either Jerusalem worse, or the north better, than their traditional reputations, we ought to remember Ezekiel's remark in his parable of Oholah and Oholibah that Jerusalem had gone to far greater lengths of depravity than her sister Samaria (Ezek. 23.4–11).[21]

Out of all this, both temple and king cast long shadows. The temple does so forward, after the exile, to the second temple and the imagery that was ultimately applied to Jesus; the king, backwards, as it were, into the past, so that his stamp is probably to be found even on the presentation of Moses and the law;[22] and forwards, too, as we shall see, into the later period when it is the person of the king who provides the pattern for the expected Messiah. Not least, Yahweh himself is described as king, and it is his kingship that becomes the kingdom of God in Judaism and in the New Testament.

We have seen something of Israelite life as it was centred on and directed towards the king and the temple. But the Old Testament presents what seemed later to be an even more dominant feature of pre-exilic Israel: the prophetic movement.

There is no question about the stature of the prophets. When estimation of the Old Testament has been at its lowest, they have still been seen as figures of deep religious and ethical insight, set into greater relief by the background against which they were contrasted. Wellhausen, as we saw, regarded them as the beginning of what was worth while in the Old Testament and it was commonplace for his contemporaries and immediate successors to see the movement as the force by which Israel rose above its surroundings. They have often been set over against cultic and ritual worship as a new 'spiritual' movement, more congenial to modern views than the attitudes they condemned.

Further study, however, has brought out much closer links between the prophets and the surroundings in which they appear, and while there is a risk that these connections may be overestimated, the probability of at least some of them warns us not to differentiate prophecy too strictly from its religious setting.

In contrast to kingship, some features in the history of prophecy can be traced, and the prophets whose words we possess appear as men with distinct features, each with a particular emphasis in the message which gives the movement its unity. Prophets were not peculiar to Israel. Parallels to Israelite prophecy can be found in records from Mari (in what is now Syria), in Egypt, in Arabia and possibly even in Phoenicia as well. In all these places we find forms of conveying divine messages which in some respects match

Israelite instances. The Old Testament knows of prophets of Baal. Prophetic guilds may well have been attached to temples. As in the case of kingship, some of these parallels are difficult to evaluate, but they are clearly relevant, especially in the early period of the monarchy. Saul meets prophets coming down from a place of worship and we find prophets in well-known cult centres: Samaria, Bethel, Gilgal, Jericho, Ramah. Elisha is sought at a sanctuary and Gad and Nathan play an active part in advising David. In I Kings 22 we find a group of prophets counselling the king and being opposed by another prophet in the name of Yahweh. The classical prophets, too, seem sometimes in conflict with another prophetic group attached to the temple.[23] All this has to be taken into account in presenting the Israelite scene.

That there is this conflict between prophets, and also that there are prophets living away from the sanctuaries reminds us not to tar them all with the same brush, but a recent study, which summarizes well the newer approach, does point up similarities:

> We cannot any longer rest content with the notion that the cultic circles of Israel and the prophetic circles were wholly separate and unrelated groups. From the earliest days of Israel's worship we are led to see that prophets appeared and delivered their oracles in close association with the sanctuaries. Many of them were in permanent association with the shrines, and were regarded as established functionaries of the cult. They delivered oracles for the benefit of those who visited the shrine and they had a particular part to play in the rites that took place. As members of the larger staff of the great temple of Jerusalem, and also no doubt of the great shrines of North Israel at Bethel and Dan, such cultic prophets had a specific function to fulfil. In these situations they developed patterns of oracular utterance, and established accepted modes of address, which formed a basis of speech forms which the canonical prophets inherited. The work of such cultic prophets is to be found at more than one point in the Psalter. ... The relationship between psalmody and prophetic utterance was one of mutual influence, not a one sided dependence of the psalmists on the prophets. As a consequence of this new appreciation of the relationship of prophecy to the cult it is clear that we cannot dismiss the attitudes of the canonical prophets to the priesthood and sanctuaries as a rejection motivated by an institutional opposition.[24]

The great prophets stand out from this background, but they are not discontinuous with it. That must be remembered. Yet, having made the statement, we must immediately qualify it in the opposite direction. For, as we have seen, it was very easy for cultic worship to become corrupt, as the prophets themselves are the first to testify, and they are the ones to criticize. The motive force behind their criticism must therefore come from somewhere else – though where that somewhere else is cannot clearly be seen, except for the prophets' affirmation that it was the call of Yahweh.

It is clear from what the prophets say and from the way in which they say it that they are not so much introducing new ideas to the people as reminding them of what they already know. Development in Israelite religion can be exaggerated, though it certainly took place. From the start there was a profound idea of God and a keen ethical consciousness which is clear from quite early material. These, however, and the Sinai covenant with which they were bound, could easily be obscured in the extravagance of the cult, the influence of surrounding Canaan and the nationalism of the court religion. The other version of the covenant, in the form which we have seen given to it with the rise of David, could add up to little more than the assurance 'God is on our side':

> It may be granted that there is evidence of a cultic tradition in Judah associated with the king which was capable of keeping alive, for those who had ears to hear, the memory of Israel's high moral code. ... It may be suspected that in actual practice most of the Judaean kings were more interested in the divine legitimization of their rule than in the moral responsibilities of kingship. Moreover, what Micah and Isaiah in their day and Zephaniah and Jeremiah a century later had to say about the popular religion and the immoral behaviour of their contemporaries would suggest that the ancient moral law was more honoured in the breach than in the observance. Indeed, cult had come to mean in Judah, as earlier in the northern kingdom, not the recollection in the sanctuary of the great decisive acts of God on behalf of his people as the ground of moral obligation, but the offering of sacrifices as a surrogate for just dealing between man and man and for considering the unfortunate and needy.[25]

The prophets attempted to bring back the depths of the old insights, adding to them a new dimension which has been introduced – again, paradoxically enough – by the best of the insights of the cult and the wise men. Their own words, detached from some of the later additions with which they are framed (see p. 47), speak more clearly than any paraphrase and should be read at first hand.

It is, however, worth pointing to the nature of the language and imagery which each one uses.[26] After the striking emergence of Amos, Isaiah in the eighth century, also from the south, says virtually nothing about the traditions of the Exodus and Sinai covenant, though he is profoundly concerned with the nature of Israel's election. He frames his message in the language of the temple worship at Jerusalem, where the vision that marks his call is set: he takes over the pictures from the psalms used in the temple and in praise of the king. Hosea reaches back through the northern traditions to the time when Yahweh called Israel out of Egypt and sees the excesses of contemporary worship as 'harlotry'. Jeremiah combines both these earlier elements and adds something more: what gives his work its distinct stamp is the way in which he himself is wholly involved in what he has to say and do. He is not just a vehicle for a pronouncement; he agonizes with all of himself over the nature of his message and whether it really is the word he has to deliver. As we shall see in the next chapter, Ezekiel and the prophet whose writing is contained in Isaiah 40–55 (not Isaiah himself, but an anonymous figure whom scholars call Second Isaiah) also use the same elements, but in a rather different way from Jeremiah and from each other. Ezekiel presents what often amounts almost to a parody on the old traditions of the Exodus as he points to the past and uses, among other things, a picture of the temple and a new covenant as images of the future. Second Isaiah looks to the future in the imagery of a new exodus, pointing to the power of Yahweh in language reminiscent of the Psalms and describing the suffering of Israel in language which probably goes back to the king's suffering at the great New Year Festival.

And what do the prophets use this imagery to say, as they couple it with their more concrete pronouncements and accusations? They look at Israel's present and at Israel's future.

It is sometimes said that the great gift of the prophets was to see deeper into their situation with a political and historical sharp-sightedness. But this is to run the same risk of misinterpretation and over-rationalization that we saw could happen in the case of the Exodus. It is probably far too modern a way of looking at things. We have to take into account, for instance, that Amos utters his prophecy of judgment before he could possibly have known that the Assyrians were on the horizon, and not as a result of that. The real strength of the prophets is not their religious interpretation of the historical scene. It is rather what we would call their religious and theological insight into the nature of the God in whom they believed. If he was what they claimed him to be, then things could not continue as they were; at some point he had to intervene.

Hence we have the prophets' message of judgment and of restoration expressed in the imagery at which we have looked all too briefly. Moreover, this message is seen to come true. That Jerusalem falls is taken by those who come after as an abundant vindication of their prophecy which also, as we shall see, provides a bridge over into a new era when traditional safeguards have gone.

The temple cult, too, looked forward to the future, though again in different terms. In practice, the future envisaged by the temple cult in the language of its festivals was one of increasing national safety and prosperity: each New Year's Festival looks forward to better things to come, and each enthronement of the king looks forward to his reign as bringing in a new age. The triumph of the 'day of Yahweh', on which God will give his people victory, is eagerly longed for. But here, too, in the future expectation, the ethical element which is so prominent a part of the prophets' message is missing, or at least submerged, in other elements. So the conflict in the present between prophet and cult is not only over the nature and practical consequences of faith in the present, but also about the nature of the future itself.

NOTES

1. 'Israelite' will be used in an ambiguous way in this chapter. Originally it is the name of the tribal alliance, but after the split between northern and southern kingdoms, it is used to refer exclusively to the north, and 'Judah' is used for the south. The context should make clear what is intended.

2. S. Mowinckel, *He That Cometh* (Oxford, 1959), p. 28.

3. *He That Cometh*, p. 34.

4. *He That Cometh*, pp. 52 ff.

5. For the question of the covenant with David, see especially R. E. Clements, *Abraham and David* (London, 1968).

6. *Abraham and David*, p. 55.

7. For more details, see e.g. R. E. Clements, *God and Temple* (Oxford, 1965), pp. 65 ff.

8. S. H. Hooke (ed.), *Myth, Ritual and Kingship* (Oxford, 1958), p. 19.

9. See especially J. H. Eaton, *The Psalms* (Torch Bible Commentary, 1967); H. Ringgren, *The Faith of the Psalmists* (London and Philadelphia, 1963).

10. See R. E. Clements, *God and Temple*, pp. 8 f.

11. In addition to *He That Cometh*, see also A. R. Johnson, *Sacral Kingship in Ancient Israel* (Cardiff, 1955, 1967[2]). References below are to the first edition.

12. *He That Cometh*, p. 69.

13. S. H. Hooke, *Myth and Ritual* (London, 1933), p. 8.

14. See H. Ringgren, *The Messiah in the Old Testament* (London, 1956), pp. 63 f.

15. See A. R. Johnson, *Sacral Kingship*, pp. 102, 108.

16. See J. R. Porter, 'The Interpretation of 2 Samuel VI and Psalm CXXXII', *Journal of Theological Studies*, 1954, pp. 151 ff.

17. S. H. Hooke, *Myth, Ritual and Kingship*, p. 20.

18. A. R. Johnson, *Sacral Kingship*, pp. 63 ff.

19. For an illuminating comparison, read S. Mowinckel, *The Psalms in Israel's Worship* (Oxford, 1962) alongside A. Weiser, *The Psalms* (London and Philadelphia, 1962).

20. See further, e.g. T. C. Vriezen, *The Religion of Ancient Israel*, pp. 186 f.

21. See S. H. Hooke, *Myth, Ritual and Kingship*, p. 18.

22. See J. R. Porter, *Moses and Monarchy* (Oxford, 1963).

23. For further details see J. Lindblom, *Prophecy in Ancient Israel*, pp. 29 f.; Vriezen, *Religion*, pp. 200 ff.

24. R. E. Clements, *Prophecy and Covenant* (London, 1965), pp. 20 f. The whole book is an excellent account of recent study of prophecy.

25. N. W. Porteous, 'The Prophets and the Problem of Continuity', in: *Israel's Prophetic Heritage*, ed. B. W. Anderson and W. Harrelson (London and New York, 1962), p. 23.

26. For a full account see G. von Rad, *The Message of the Prophets* (London, 1968).

6 Hopes for the Future

In 587 BC the world that we have been looking at came to a sudden end. A Babylonian force under Nebuchadnezzar captured and destroyed Jerusalem, devastated the country-side and carried away the leading inhabitants of Jerusalem into exile in Babylon. It is difficult to estimate the extent of the destruction and upheaval at all accurately; perhaps it was less than that experienced by the northern kingdom in 721 when a very considerable resettlement took place. Nor is it easy to estimate just what physical conditions were like in the exile as we have so little evidence to go by; it is doubtful whether we should think of anything so drastic as wide-scale imprisonment.[1]

On the other hand, the psychological effect of the exile can hardly be put too strongly. For this was the destruction of Jerusalem and the Jerusalem temple, which had come to stand for so much, and an end to the independent nation and its old way of life. Something of the shock is preserved for us in the writings of those who went through this collapse and whose work is still preserved: the book entitled the Lamentations of Jeremiah and Psalm 137 speak for themselves, but even this will not represent the full depths of the catastrophe. For these writings have been preserved by those who had to some degree come through and who could set them in a context which interpreted even the final horror in terms of the God they knew. For lesser people, what had happened would often have been the end of their faith. From the words of those who did come through, we can see pictures of their weaker contemporaries turning to other gods and objects of worship and even transferring their allegiance to the gods of Babylonia whom they felt to have been victorious.[2]

But despite the shock, even the destruction of Jerusalem and the loss of a way of life could be taken up and incorporated in the faith of those who still worshipped Yahweh. This was not least because this destruction had actually been foretold, as we saw in the previous chapter, by prophetic critics of the former state of affairs and because the threat of judgment had, as far as we can see, also held out hope of a happier issue, provided that a proper response was made.

This view does not seem to have been confined to the prophets. Even before the exile, we see another movement which expresses itself along these lines. Its programme can be found in the book of Deuteronomy. Deuteronomy and the prophetic movement are not independent of each other, but their relationship is certainly indirect, and needs to be discussed in more detail than is possible here.

Deuteronomy appears, according to the Old Testament, against a background of religious and political reform, the chief cause of which seems to be a new wave of nationalism, under King Josiah (646–609) of Judah, made possible by a crisis in the position of the dominating power, Assyria. Just how what we may call the Deuteronomic movement was related to Josiah's reform need not concern us here. It is enough to point to the probability that the movement goes back considerably before Josiah's time and that although it comes to expression in Jerusalem and has in mind the religious situation there, its roots are to be found in the North, among the old tribal traditions.[3] Nor need we go into the question of the exact relationship between the events described in II Kings 22 and 23 and the book of Deuteronomy as we now have it. Here again, the evidence is awkwardly circular. The events described have been written up so as to point to the present Deuteronomy; its perspective on the account of the finding of the book, therefore, may well be different from that which would be held at the time of the events recorded. So the link between our Deuteronomy and the earlier book may be even more complex than has so far been suggested.[4] That Deuteronomy goes back to a movement in the time of Josiah, however, we need not doubt; and this movement, too, was capable of transformation over the difficult period of the exile.

Deuteronomy takes the people whom it addresses back to the time when they were on the verge of entering the land which they had been promised, thus bringing back the old tribal traditions sharply into prominence. Its structure and content are strongly marked by the old covenant associated with Sinai. To the assembled people the law is presented almost in the form of a sermon, with warnings as to what will happen if it is disobeyed, and with promises of the good that will come to an obedient people.[5] But we have more than a re-presentation of past history. The old pattern is reinterpreted in line with the needs of the present, in Jerusalem.

Of course, Jerusalem is not mentioned by name; but it is there all the same. It will be remembered that the old amphictyony had a central shrine, as a focal point for the alliance. Behind the message of Deuteronomy is the intention to make Jerusalem, and Jerusalem alone, this central shrine. In the earlier period the central shrine had only been one among others, but now the detrimental influence of Canaanite practices on Israelite worship has made it necessary for a harsher attitude to be adopted – as is clear from statements throughout the book, Jerusalem is to be the only place of worship.

But the choice of Jerusalem could lead to misunderstanding of its status. The traditions associated with it that we examined in the previous chapter show how easily a 'Jerusalem mystique' could attach to temple and king. The authors of Deuteronomy thus took an immensely important step:

Jerusalem, Mount Zion and its temple were all 'demythologized', and in place of the older mythology, by which Yahweh's abode on earth was thought to be united to his abode in heaven, the Deuteronomists offered a theological concept which expressed the manner of Yahweh's dwelling upon earth. This was that of Yahweh's name, which was set in the place which he had chosen. The invocation and public proclamation of the divine name had played a vital part in the worship of early Israel, and now this was elevated still further, so that the name of Yahweh was made the vehicle of his presence. It was his *alter ego*, by means of which he had made himself present to men, without ever leaving his heavenly dwelling place. For the first time, therefore, we have with the Deuteronomists a strictly theological endeavour to express the reality of Yahweh's presence within Israel, which did not throw in question his heavenly and transcendent nature. In the earlier Jerusalem tradition the meaning of Yahweh's temple and the manner of his dwelling there had been explained on the basis of mythology in which things on earth and things in heaven were believed to be mysteriously related. Deuteronomy now broke with this mythology and replaced it with a theology in which the divine name became the means by which the transcendent Yahweh was present with his people. By this re-interpretation the Deuteronomists hoped to preclude the idea that Yahweh was contained in the natural order, as a part of a natural chain of cause and effect, and to assert beyond question that he was superior to all his creation. His dwelling within Israel was thereby stressed as a gift of grace.[6]

The value of this interpretation for a time when the temple no longer existed and in the vastly changed circumstances of the exile and its aftermath needs hardly to be stressed.

In addition to the law book Deuteronomy, there was also a reinterpretation of Israelite history determined by similar theological motives. We have already come across this reinterpretation in the books stretching from Joshua to II Kings, as rather tedious editorial material which prevented us from getting back to the earlier traditions for which we were searching. Now it is time to see it in its proper perspective, as a new reading of the past in the light of the present, quite as important and creative as that of the Yahwist in an earlier period. Once again, it is difficult to know whether the Deuteronomic history writing is the work of one author or several; if it is by one person, he is writing in a tradition.[7]

The first part of the work, up to the establishment of the monarchy in Jerusalem, has, as we have seen, less editorial comment than the second, and this indicates the Deuteronomist's interest. In this first half we have a pattern of renewed failure on the part of Israel, followed by intervention and aid from Yahweh in the form of a deliverer. This leads to the need for something more lasting and so the monarchy is instituted. Here, the various traditions are now so interpreted as to indicate that the monarchy is both a human institution, under divine judgment, and also a divinely ordained medium of divine grace. Alongside this runs the establishment of the true shrine, for as one after another of the great religious centres of the earlier period is shown to be no longer the one chosen, the choosing of Jerusalem, intimately connected with the establishment of true monarchy, makes the way clear for the building of the shrine which embodies that willingness of God to make his dwelling in the midst of the people.[8]

But the pattern of failure and subsequent need for renewal sets in once again, in the stereotyped verdicts on king after king, each of whom is judged by his attitude to law and temple, rather than for his political achievements. The north falls, and its fall is seen as a last warning for the south to mend its ways. But the warning is not heeded. Judgment comes.

But it is *God's* judgment, the judgment of the God who chose Israel in the first place. And this God is not confined to land or temple, but is the God who dwells in heaven; it is the God, too, who promised an eternal covenant. Despite the judgment, therefore, there is hope. The people still have a chance to return.

Shortly after the construction of the Deuteronomic history work and parallel to it, or perhaps succeeding it in purpose, comes another great structure built up on not dissimilar lines. Because of the material it uses and its attitude it is known as the Priestly Writing. Like Deuteronomy, it has both law and narrative, and contains material which is extremely old, some of it written material. It should probably be put in the exilic period, too, and it is generally thought to have been produced in Babylonia. As was pointed out in an earlier chapter, however, it was added to and altered over a considerable period afterwards (see pp. 45f.). Again, whether we should attribute it to a single author or several authors is uncertain.[9]

As with the book of Deuteronomy, we are transported back into the wilderness, but this time the wilderness is where the narrative also ends. There is no move on into the Promised Land. Instead of taking the form of a re-presentation of events between the covenant on Sinai and the time of composition, the narrative of the Priestly Writing is a reinterpretation of events from the very beginning of the world to the arrival of Israel on the verge of the territory they are to occupy. We therefore have an alternative to much of the account of the Yahwist (and Elohist) with whose writing the work was eventually combined.

The opening account of creation finds a climax in the sabbath rest of God after the creation, which is a first indication of the interests of the Priestly writer. The relationship between God and his chosen people and its basic character is thus established at the very foundation of the world. But this is only the beginning. The narrative moves on to describe two covenants, which give shape to the whole work. The first covenant comes after the flood, and is made with Noah. It is a promise never again to destroy the earth and is signed and sealed in the symbol of the rainbow. The second covenant is made with Abraham and promises to him and his descendants the land of Canaan and God's own presence in their midst. This time the symbol used to seal the covenant is that of circumcision.

This element of promise is paramount, and must be set firmly beside the mass of legislation so evident in the rest of the work for the view of the Priestly writer to be seen properly. The law is provided by God as the means by which the promise may be fulfilled. It is not a means on its own; its place is in a context among a people to whom the promise has already been given.

It is interesting to see that when the Priestly Writing comes to the events at Sinai, there is no mention of a covenant. Sinai is concerned rather with the fulfilment on both sides of the promise which has already been given. It therefore consists in the promulgation of laws which will indeed make it possible for God to dwell in the midst of Israel. In this section, earlier laws are taken up and put in a new setting. For we must remember that it is as it were at Sinai that the real people of Israel, for whom the Priestly Writing has been composed, now are; they have yet to reach their promised land. They, too, stand outside it in a country which is not theirs, and their position is worse than that of their ancestors, for they have already suffered the disasters of disobedience and must learn the lesson all over again.

Like the Deuteronomic History, the Priestly Writing reflects in its presentation the changes which occurred between the original Sinai and its re-enactment. Once again the temple forms a powerful influence. The tabernacle which is the place where God wills to dwell, and whose making takes up most of the second half of the book of Exodus, is a reconstruction, in suitably portable form, of the temple at Jerusalem.[10] Features of the structure of the temple and its furnishings are associated with a tent sanctuary which goes back far into Israelite tradition, to produce a place where God may meet his people.

The lack of permanence is deliberate. God is not bound to a fixed place on earth for his dwelling. Indeed, as in the writings of the Deuteronomists, his presence is mediated. In this case, however, it is not his name, but his glory which comes to be the mode of his presence. In complete accord with this view of the nature of God, the significance of the cultic acts of which the Priestly Writing is so full are also changed. Whereas in pre-exilic times there was a view that the performance of the cult was in itself in some way efficacious, the Priestly writer sees its actions as symbols, which serve to communicate God's grace.

Israel is no longer a nation with a king, and the terminology again reflects this fact. The people are described as a congregation and the supreme figure is the High Priest. It seems that many of the items of dress traditionally worn by kings have been, once more, 'demythologized' and transferred to him.

All this, as will have become clear, is not only a reinterpretation of the past in the light of the present, but also a programme for the future. How the Priestly Writing ends we do not know, but it is possible that it includes the details of the apportionment of the land given in the second half of the book of Joshua. But there is no conquest.[11] For the Priestly Writing, everything is firmly in God's hands. His was the judgment, and in his everlasting covenant lies the hope for the future, if it is to come:

The Deuteronomic history shows failure for what it is and warns that these are the consequences of men's refusal to accept the promises of God and to respond in the right conduct which marks the people of God. The Priestly Work shows the uncertainty. . . . It traces failure right back into the very beginnings of life – for now it has taken into itself, too, that initial failure by which all creation was put out of joint. It leaves its readers and hearers on the edge of the land, knowing that the land can be theirs – for so the familiar history would tell them. Now they are away from it, amid alien life. The question whether history can repeat itself remains open, but the issue is not really in doubt, because just as once Egypt could know that 'I am Yahweh', so once again the aliens among whom they dwell will be able to know. God will again bring them in, he will again meet with them.[12]

In the previous chapter we left the prophets pointing predominantly to the threat of Yahweh's judgment, in contrast to the more superficially optimistic attitude prevailing elsewhere. At the same time, however, there were hints at the possibility of better things if the people changed their ways. Now the judgment has indeed come, and the emphasis shifts to restoration and hope. This can be seen particularly clearly at the end of the book of Ezekiel, who was mentioned briefly in passing; and at the same time it becomes clear how near prophecy now comes to the ideas of the renewal of Israel coming from other sources.

Ezekiel does not transfer his hope into the past. There is no hope there. In the past, Yahweh had mercy on Israel as a newborn baby, unwashed and unloved, exposed in open country still weltering in the blood and slime in which it had been born. The revolting object was saved by Yahweh, and grew to be his beautiful bride, but there was hidden corruption, and the bride became a promiscuous harlot (Ezekiel 16; see ch. 23). The imagery of Israel's traditions of election are turned into caricatures. There is no hope there; it must come from what Yahweh is. In Ezekiel, who has himself been shattered by the judgment, the significance of the disaster has bitten deep.[13]

His hope therefore is put explicitly in the form of a future picture of a new city and a new temple in a purified land. There are similarities to the Priestly Writing, and there are differences. Here, too, God is related to the people by his 'glory': the glory which departed at the fall of Jerusalem is to return to dwell among the people again. There are the same instructions to be followed in the people's worship, to ensure its purity. There is the same idealized reconstruction of the temple. But the divine grace of God is stressed even more strongly. We do not have the new sanctuary constructed by human helpers as they are listed in the Priestly Writing. Human sharing in the task is left unmentioned. Divine action also reorders the land and gives it a new geography and settles the people in a new way. And with the return of God, a stream – that stream which we saw as part of the imagery of Jerusalem in the previous chapter – flows from his temple bringing life from Yahweh to his land.[14]

A change in the features of the land is also part of the vision of Second Isaiah (as it is of other visions of a restored Israel of this period and later). Jerusalem is to be lifted up, and the land round it levelled to provide a pathway on which the exiles can return. For Second Isaiah, writing when he does, the end is in sight. The judgment is over; the penalty is paid. Only the one joyful message needs to be given: 'We're going home.' The people in exile have begun to doubt whether this moment will ever come and they have been tempted in the direction of the gods of Babylonia. But what are these, compared with Yahweh? The time of doubt and despair can really end.

What Yahweh is about to do is described in terms of the creation of the world and of the Exodus, two events which had already been linked together in worship at the temple before the exile. There is to be a new victory over the forces of chaos and a new deliverance of the chosen people from captivity. But this imagery only serves as a symbol, a pointer of what is to come. Creation and Exodus are former things which are to be remembered, in that they are hints of the power of the God who brought them about; yet at the same time they will be able to be forgotten, because what is about to happen will eclipse them completely.[15] We find no detailed programme of what the new things will be; there is nothing to parallel what we saw in the Priestly Writing or

Ezekiel. This lack of detail, however, leaves room for the stressing of a point which, though made elsewhere, is never brought out as clearly as it is in these chapters. It could seem that the hopes of Israel were limited to its people alone. But that is not so. What is done in and for Israel is set in the context of the whole world. Israel is to return and to serve God in a new life, so that all the nations of the world can see God's glory through Israel and come to prostrate themselves before him, too.

Such are the hopes of the exiles. But how far are they fulfilled?

To see just what happened we have to rely a good deal on the evidence of the Chronicler, the writer (or – it must be said again – writers) responsible for the two books of Chronicles, Ezra and Nehemiah. What has been said about the other great 'historical' works of the Old Testament applies equally here, too; once again the Chronicler makes use of old material, but he does not make use of it for strictly historical purposes. His is a theological work, again picturing the past in terms of, and as leading up to, his present (and once again the original work has been changed with the addition of later material). We shall see later what his purpose was in writing; but this purpose makes it the more difficult to trace the historical sequence underlying the account.

The exiles did, of course, return with the capture of Babylon by Cyrus, though probably not quite as promptly as the Chronicler suggests. This resettlement was in line with Persian policy. But just how the return took place is more difficult to tell. In terms of the imagery we have just seen, what more glorious than to return home, to restore the place where God would dwell among his people? And so the Chronicler thought. The way home was free, the people were eager and willing to return. In the event, however, the reality fell short of the vision and the response was far from enthusiastic.[16]

By this time many of the exiles had made new lives in Babylon and seem to have been reasonably comfortable; the journey back was long and a good deal of hard work lay ahead. The numbers involved in the first return were probably small, and perhaps because Persian control was not properly established in Palestine, it seems to have come up against serious difficulties.

The next stage is slightly clearer, as we have two prophetic books, Haggai and Zechariah (in part), which supplement and help to control the Chronicler's story. Even those who did return seem to have been less than enthusiastic about the rebuilding of the temple and more concerned for their own well-being. Haggai gives a picture of reluctance to rebuild and sees failure of crops and low morale as a result of the neglect. This picture provides a kind of negative correlation to the ideals we saw earlier. Blessing on the land is closely related with the restoration of the place which God, though heaven cannot contain him, has nevertheless chosen as his dwelling place. Passages in Zechariah are illuminated by this same approach. God will come if only the people will respond.[17]

Just as the temple is connected with the new age, so, too, is a successor of the king. Zerubbabel, a rather mysterious figure, of the line of David, is talked of in imagery which designates him a ruler in the age of blessing. What happened to him is obscure, as the text may well have undergone later editing, but the type of expectation is an important prelude to a development we shall see shortly.

After these events, belonging at the end of the sixth century, comes a gap which takes us well towards the end of the fifth century and even into the fourth. Here again the work of the Chronicler, which is our only source, causes difficulties. His account of the reforming work of Ezra and Nehemiah is almost certainly not as he originally left it. Even a superficial reading shows a lack of connection between Ezra and Nehemiah, although they are working together at apparently the same period. The best solution to the problem of the arrangement of the material as we have it seems to be that the memoirs of Nehemiah, much of which is in the first person, were wrongly associated with the time of Ezra and placed in the context of the Ezra material, wherever it seemed to fit best. Thus although in the present account Ezra seems to precede Nehemiah, historically the sequence was the other way round. But whatever the historical problems, here, too, we see a continuation of the attempts at the purification of Israel's worship which reach back to before the exile.[18]

Ezra stands on the boundary between the end of the Old Testament record and the beginning of Jewish legend about the origin of the Law and his work is about as difficult to assess as that of Moses, with whom he is so often compared. That he took measures to reform and reorganize the community once again is clear and his association with the Law must also hold, though it is not easy to assess the Chronicler's account as it now stands. The dangers of isolationism are plain enough, but in the atmosphere of the time there would have been no other means of survival.

And so, lastly, we come to the Chronicler himself and the theological standpoint from which he presents the events to whose historical reality we have tried to penetrate.[19] That it has proved so difficult is not least because the Chronicler sits almost more lightly to history than most of his predecessors. Probably starting from an abridged version of the Deuteronomic history, he outlines the development from creation to his day, but the way in which this development is presented shows clearly his own interests. Little more than one long genealogy takes us from Adam to the death of Saul; then a treatment of David's reign follows which leaves us in no doubt that here is the Chronicler's ideal. After David, it is the reforming figures who are made to stand out most clearly: Hezekiah and Josiah before the exile and Ezra after it. The attitude of the Deuteronomists is taken over and exaggerated even further; divine grace and judgment are emphasized even more strongly so that sheer idealism takes the place of history. What used to be rooted in history is torn free. Human conflict – even war – and human activity become submerged in a constant round of worship, and preparation and purification for worship.

Not that all this is without a purpose, for here now – and

not in the realm of politics – lies the concern of the Chronicler's own community:

> It is the great contribution of the Chronicler that he takes up on the one hand the themes of the Deuteronomic Historian and traces their further development in the later period; and at the same time he takes up the Priestly concern with purity and legitimacy and right organization. He links these, not in a simple re-presentation of the way in which historical experience has become theological experience. The community is shown that the real values of the past are enshrined in the present, that Davidic monarchy and all that it betokens of divine grace is exemplified in temple and cultus, that a community joined in the joyous worship of God, a community purified and renewed, is the recipient of divine promise.[20]

Our long survey is almost over, but in conclusion there are two developments which must be introduced briefly to complete the picture.

The first is the question of the Jewish future hope, its expectation of the action of God still to come. We have seen this expectation in the judgment pronounced by the prophets, the programmes of restoration and the hopes pinned on the return. In all this much was longed for, and what happened in reality fell short of the vision:

> The hope attached to Zerubbabel came to nothing. The actual conditions after the return were but a feeble realization of Deutero-Isaiah's glorious promises. Thereafter the hope of restoration deliberately looks forward to a future not yet to hand, and gradually discards the connexion which the royal ideology previously had with cultic empirical experience.[21]

Here is the beginning of hope in the kingdom of God, the kingdom which in some versions of this hope is ruled by the Messiah, the anointed one, as God's agent. It is from this beginning, and influenced, too, by other sources, that the vivid world of Jewish apocalyptic develops and forms the background to the beginnings of Christianity alongside other elements in Judaism.[22] And perhaps there is more than unrealized hope at work here:

> It seems probable that we should understand the concept of an ideal Davidic ruler – a Messiah in the technical sense – as arising not simply out of the failure of the pre-exilic Davidic monarchy, but out

of the embodiment in it of the reality of what it was intended or believed to be. For what likelihood is there that an institution adjudged to have been an utter failure will provide the picture of an ideal future? So too the projection into the future of the hopes of a new age is not simply a matter of dissatisfaction with the present, disillusionment as a result of the deferment of hope. It is a recognition rather of the fulness of what is already tasted as reality. The prophets of the restoration period were both idealists and realists; as such they were able to see in the realities of a not very encouraging situation the earnest of what they believed to be present, namely a new age with the glory of God at the very centre of the community's life.[23]

The second brings us back to the figures with whom we began: the wise men. With the Exile, wisdom as we saw it earlier breaks down – or develops, for the process can be seen in either way. Wisdom, we noted, was primarily concerned with everyday life; confronted by the magnitude of the exile, this form of thinking had to undergo change within the context of Israelite belief. It could turn to a weary scepticism – and that is what we see in Ecclesiastes; but taken up with the other traditions it could be transformed and transform the traditions themselves in the process. Much of what we have been looking at can be seen as the work of wise men, just as the Yahwist's work could be put in this category:

The idea of history created, as it seems, in the reign of David, was maintained by the later scribes who found themselves faced with the task of answering almost the opposite question: how had Israel fallen under the judgment of Yahweh? The question could be answered only by an appeal to experience; and experience here included the prophetic interpretation of events. The words of the prophets had been vindicated by experience, and nothing but these words gave an insight into the catastrophe which had befallen Israel. ... The scribes were not limited to the traditional wisdom. They had learned another scribal principle, that the wise man has a fund of wise sayings for any situation, and that these wise sayings should reflect collective experience. The sayings of the prophets furnished the pertinent wise sayings, and they too should be collected and preserved.[24]

This interpretation can be paralleled, as the apocryphal books of Ecclesiasticus and the Wisdom of Solomon

suggest, at the end of the Old Testament period in the understanding of the Old Testament canon itself:

> As the Israelite became increasingly aware of his dislocation from a
> history providing the primary clue to Yahweh's sovereignty, he saw
> that sovereignty in terms of the wisdom through which his individual
> existence in the cosmos found meaning beyond and in spite of the
> brokenness of Israel's communal historicity. It was against such a
> background that the Israelite came to a new statement of the mean-
> ing of the book, the canon, that his broken history had left in his
> hand. The Law and the Prophets came to be read as wisdom litera-
> ture was read, as wise men read the double genre of tale and
> instruction, as the literature of wisdom *par excellence*, as *the* truth
> about the nature of things. Wisdom had come to be a synonym of
> *torah*, Law, and what a poem such as Psalm 119 celebrates as that
> which must be the subject of continual meditation – the *torah* of
> Yahweh – is really the same thing being praised in Proverbs 8 and 9.
> So it was that the narrative from Adam to Moses came to be seen
> as a wisdom tale certifying the validity of the Mosaic instruction
> set down in Exodus, Leviticus, Numbers, and Deuteronomy. So it
> was that the narrative from Joshua to Jehoiachin became the tale
> preceding the instruction to be found in the corpus of the latter
> prophets from Isaiah to Malachi. So it was that the Law and the
> Prophets as a whole became the tale preceding the predominantly
> didactic materials included in the final section of the Hebrew canon,
> the Writings. . . . So it was that prophecy gave way to apocalyptic,
> the detailed literary visions of which are in terms of their basic genre
> but the eschatological counterpart of the collections of wisdom
> literature.[25]

Here we are brought to another place where wisdom has
been influential: the book of Daniel, whose conduct
reminds us of that of Joseph in an earlier account. We could
go on to discuss the book of Job, the climax of the wisdom
literature in the narrower sense, which in turn may well also
reflect the experience of Israel in undergoing the exile.[26] But
there is room for no more.

Nevertheless, perhaps even this briefest of sketches has
shown the richness, variety and profundity of the Old
Testament, not least in the post-exilic period in which it
finally took shape. Some facts are now before us. It remains
to consider at last the question with which this book began.
What about the Old Testament?

NOTES

1. For further details see Bright, *History of Israel*, pp. 323 ff.; Noth, *History of Israel*, pp. 299 ff.; P. R. Ackroyd, *Exile and Restoration* (London and Philadelphia, 1968), pp. 17 ff.

2. *Exile and Restoration*, pp. 39 ff.

3. For further details see E. W. Nicholson, *Deuteronomy and Tradition* (Oxford, 1967); R. E. Clements, *God and Temple*, pp. 88 f.

4. *Exile and Restoration*, p. 68.

5. See R. E. Clements, *God's Chosen People* (London, 1968).

6. R. E. Clements, *God and Temple*, pp. 94 f.

7. For an excellent survey, see *Exile and Restoration*, pp. 62 ff.

8. *Exile and Restoration*, p. 74.

9. See *Exile and Restoration*, pp. 84 ff.; *God and Temple*, pp. 100 ff.

10. For details, see Martin Noth, *Exodus* (London and Philadelphia, 1962).

11. See *Exile and Restoration*, p. 97.

12. *Exile and Restoration*, p. 102.

13. For a commentary on Ezekiel see D. M. G. Stalker, *Ezekiel* (Torch Bible Commentaries, 1968); see also G. von Rad, *The Message of the Prophets* (London, 1968), pp. 189 ff.

14. See *God and Temple*, pp. 103 ff.; *Exile and Restoration*, pp. 103 ff.

15. See *The Message of the Prophets*, pp. 206 ff.; *Exile and Restoration*, pp. 118 ff.; and for a fine commentary, C. Westermann, *Isaiah 40–66* (London, 1969).

16. See *Exile and Restoration*, pp. 138 ff.; *God and Temple*, 123 ff., for what follows.

17. See *Exile and Restoration*, pp. 153 ff.

18. For more detail, see e.g. Bright, *History of Israel*, pp. 356 ff.

19. For this section, see P. R. Ackroyd, 'History and Theology in the Writings of the Chronicler', *Concordia Theological Monthly* 38 (1967), pp. 501 ff.

20. Ackroyd, 'The Chronicler', p. 515.

21. S. Mowinckel, *He That Cometh*, p. 156.

22. For a useful short guide see D. S. Russell, *Between the Testaments* (London, 1965); also, his *The Jews from Alexander to Herod* (London, 1967).

23. *Exile and Restoration*, pp. 253 f.

24. J. L. McKenzie, 'Reflections on Wisdom', *Journal of Biblical Literature*, LXXXVI (1967), pp. 7 f.

25. H. H. Guthrie, *Wisdom and Canon: Meanings of the Law and the Prophets* (Evanston, 1966), p. 27.

26. *Exile and Restoration*, pp. 245 ff.

7   What about the Old Testament?

Before we began to survey the contents of the Old Testament against their historical background we had come up against a conflict. By modern critical and scientific-historical standards, the history of the Old Testament in Judaism, and perhaps even more in Christianity, could be seen as the history of a type of interpretation which read more than was warranted into the text of the Old Testament. We saw how, right from the beginning, some Christians standing outside the main tradition failed to see the same significance in the Old Testament and rejected it; how the problem they felt seemed to become increasingly acute with the rise of criticism from the eighteenth century onwards; and how recent years have seen either widespread revolt against, or apathy towards, the Old Testament. A quotation from the famous church historian Adolf von Harnack, who wrote a study of Marcion, one of the first Christians to reject the Old Testament, sums up the position very much as we left it:

> To reject the Old Testament in the second century was a mistake which the Church rightly repudiated; to retain it in the sixteenth century was a fate which the Reformation could not yet avoid; but to continue to keep it in Protestantism as a canonical document after the nineteenth century is the consequence of religious and ecclesiastical paralysis. . . . To sweep the table clean and honour the truth in confession and teaching is the action required of Protestantism today. And it is almost too late.[1]

What about the Old Testament? Was Harnack right? Should the table be swept clean?

It is now time to look for an answer. But before we do, the question has to be made rather more precise. If we ask, 'What about the Old Testament?' meaning, 'What is the place of the Old Testament in Christianity?' we must immediately go on to add the further question, 'For what?' Are we concerned about the place of the Old Testament as a book that is read regularly in church services, or as a book which is part of a syllabus of religious education, or as a book which is one of the foundations of Christian theology, or as holy, inspired, authoritative Scripture?

Often the question of the Old Testament is raised as though an answer could be given to it quite separately, without affecting the status and use of the New Testament. There seems to be a not uncommon belief that the Old Testament should and could be dropped as being a sub-Christian work, but that the retention of the New Testament poses no problems. A gradual separation of the New Testament from the Old is coming about; sometimes deliberate, sometimes almost accidental. Some theologians deliberately take up a negative attitude to the Old Testament, contrasting it as law over against promise, regarding it as a negative history of failure, a primitive background for which other pre- or non-Christian religions could be substituted with little loss. Far more influential, however, has been the way in which translations have been made of the New Testament only (or of the New Testament first, to be followed by the Old after a considerable interval). There are obvious practical and commercial reasons for this, but the result has been to give the New Testament an apparent (and perhaps misleading) immediacy which is not extended to the Old, and which thus seems to put the two books on different planes.

The danger here is a serious one. What we have is nothing less than a misunderstanding of the character of the New Testament and an illegitimate and unconsidered separation of it from the Old Testament. Marcion, who made a more fully thought out attempt to jettison the Old Testament in favour of what was to become the New, showed greater awareness of what such a course involved. Dropping the Old Testament also meant dropping half the New Testament as well; for the roots of the New Testament lie firmly in the Old, making the connection between the two very close indeed. Not only does the New Testament take up much of the imagery of the Old Testament and reinterpret it in the light of further events; as the customary Christian titles of the books show, the New Testament has been formed on the model of the Old. If the Old Testament were to be allowed to slip away from Christianity, a new problem would arise to demand an eventual answer. How is the New Testament to be interpreted and its status justified if it is left in solitary isolation?[2]

Fortunately, however, that is an issue that we need not examine further, because it still does not get to the heart of the matter. A far more pressing problem is the one which has been raised implicitly by the way in which we have been looking at the Old Testament in the previous chapters. Just what are we to make of the whole idea of Holy Scripture, of the Bible as a divinely inspired, uniquely authoritative book, in the light of the modern critical approach?

A wide variety of Christian theological traditions and approaches begins from the presupposition that the Bible is the Word of God, and that the primary – possibly even the only – question of importance is how it should be interpreted to different historical and cultural audiences. These approaches vary considerably in sophistication. There is what is most often called the 'fundamentalist' approach, which insists, despite all the difficulties that we have seen, on maintaining the Bible as an infallibly inspired source of divine teaching.[3] There can be a less rigorous 'evangelical' approach which, while not maintaining so strict a position on infallibility, still insists that the Bible and the Bible alone is the Christian norm. Then there is the kind of approach which has long gone under the name of 'biblical theology' – though like all labels that is not wholly appropriate – which lays great emphasis on the importance of recovering authentic biblical concepts and determining their significance, at the same time regarding the perspective on the world thus gained as being normative. There are modern versions of the earlier allegorical interpretation of the Bible, this time presented as 'typology' and the working out of a 'sensus plenior'.[4] There is the interpretative method known as 'demythologizing', in practice applied almost exclusively to the New Testament, which interprets the allegedly mythological statements of the New Testament in terms of human experience by means of the concepts of existentialist theology.[5] And, finally, there is the rapidly developing new interest in biblical hermeneutics, the method of interpreting the Bible as the Word of God so that it speaks to a scientific civilization.[6] All these are very different approaches and there is much dispute over their respective merits, but underlying each of them is the basic presupposition of the special status of the Bible as the material that is being interpreted.

But why should the Bible be given this special status? Why should it be set on its own in what can be almost a timeless context? In our survey of the greater part of it, we have found the Bible to be a book like any other book, the origins of which could be traced in the same way as any other book. We also saw that the Bible cannot be properly and fully understood unless it is set against a particular *historical* context because it is the account of certain experiences and insights and happenings among a particular people at particular times. (Perhaps it should be stressed, to avoid misunderstanding, that these comments refer to the characteristics of the Bible as a book and are not intended to pass judgment on the character and significance of the ideas, events and people which make up the content of the Bible.)

As we have looked at the Old Testament in this way, we have seen it to be as it were open-ended, or rather, as was said above, we have seen the focus of attention shift from a book to a people and the course of their way of life. This is the change which has been brought about by the modern approach, and its full significance has probably still to be realized.

An illustration may help here:

In a lecture given in Oxford in 1945 Dr Charles Raven described the coming of modern scientific theory as being due to a turning from dependence on the dicta of acknowledged authorities in the past to study of the data provided by the natural world in the present. He showed how modern zoology began when, instead of relying on Aristotelian and heraldic representations of animals in traditional bestiaries, men based their research on the observation of the actual nature and behaviour of living creatures. . . .

As a result of this last century's biblical studies, we are at a similar turning-point in the history of Christian theology. These studies have mainly been concerned with exegesis, that is to say, with attempts to discover the authorship and origin of the various books or parts of books, the historical circumstances in which they were produced, and what they must have meant to their authors and first readers. We now know a great deal more than our forefathers, not only about dates and origins, but also about what kind of people were these writers and the people they wrote about, what would have been their ways of thinking in their respective ages and cultures. We have not yet fully realized how radical a revolution this involves in our way of understanding the biblical revelation. A hundred years ago our forefathers looked to the Bible in the same way that mediaeval zoologists looked to Aristotle and heraldic bestiaries. To their successors' substituting of observation of actual animals corresponds our attention to the historical provenance of the biblical writings. But we have not yet shaken ourselves free from the habit of trying to look for our own guidance to some authoritative voice in the past.[7]

There is still dispute over the propriety of the approach we have made, but for the purposes of this book it is quite enough to leave it with the status of a hypothesis. Does this approach help to illuminate problems which hinder the understanding of the Old Testament? Does it do justice to things as they seem to be? Does it show the way forward for future hypotheses? The reader may safely judge for himself. A far more important issue is the question of authority, with which we are engaged.

The reason given for the special status of the Bible is that it occupies its distinctive place as a result of the Church's decision, like that of Judaism earlier in the case of the Old Testament, that here was a definitive record and criterion:

The canon is the church's way of pointing to the sacred writings in which it has heard the voice of God and marking them off from all other writings, religious and secular alike, as the ones that are uniquely the means of God's revelation.[8]

But is this not, for us, at any rate, a position which raises a considerable number of questions? It is, of course, a matter of history that at particular points in time Judaism and the Christian Church accorded the Old Testament and the Christian Bible canonical status. We can see the reasons which led to the decisions and appreciate how the process of canonization came about. But are the decision and its consequences irreversible? Are they not open to possible questioning and re-examination, not so much in order to put between the covers of what we call 'The Bible' a different selection of books (which would be pointless because the formation of the Bible is a matter of history which cannot now be re-opened), but to reassess the position the Bible should now occupy?

As a matter of practice, such a reappraisal does go on, somewhat haphazardly, in the churches' everyday use of the Bible. The time is past for almost all Christians, when decision was a matter of 'the Bible says'. Even in the most fundamentalist circles some criterion of selection, some attempt at complete reinterpretation in places, characterizes the use of the Bible. Parts of it are stressed, parts are totally ignored. The canon is too big; it has parts which cannot be used. There is a 'canon within the canon'. Whether this sees the real question clearly enough, however, is another matter.

For other purposes, for understanding the meaning of the Bible in its context, what Judaism and the Church have preserved for us is far too little to satisfy our needs. The eagerness with which scholars struggle to interpret works contemporary to the Bible and now preserved only in Ethiopic or Slavonic, the meticulous piecing together of broken papyri, the energy spent on assessing the Dead Sea Scrolls or the Targum Neofiti or the Coptic Gnostic works from Nag Hammadi and their significance for Christian origins, show how keen the thirst is for more material. What would we not give for some of the works replaced by the later forms that we have in the Bible: the suppressed passages of the Yahwist (and the Elohist), the sources behind I and II Kings, the mysterious 'Q', the material from which Luke wrote the Acts of the Apostles? Anything from the past, whether 'orthodox' or 'heretical', gives us more illumination of the way in which Christianity developed, and it is impossible not to regret some of the treasures which have been suppressed in the course of action which lay behind the process of forming the canon.

But there is no point in wasting time on historical 'might-have-beens'. The mere fact that we find historical back-ground important in our understanding of the Bible shows how Christian thought and judgment today are formed by a more complex process than the last quotation implied. A recent study of the principles of Christian theology singled out six factors which determine the character of Christian thinking and its approach to our present situation: ex-perience, revelation, scripture, tradition, culture, reason.[9] Scripture is an important element in this complex, but it is not the only one. Indeed, when it is made absolute it runs the risk of damaging the balance which has to be maintained between the factors:

> Exaggeration of one or other of the formative factors must lead to theological distortion. Too much stress on experience is the cause of individualism, enthusiasm and, at the worst, fanaticism. A too rigid emphasis on revelation, and on the scripture and tradition which mediate it, leads to obscurantism, antiquarianism, ultra-conservatism. Those who lean too far in the direction of accommodating theology to the mood of the culture or of trying to exhaust its content in terms of what can be rationally established apart from religious experience and revelation end up with a shallow modernism or rationalism from which the distinctive religious content has been eliminated.[10]

The way in which the Church does not in practice accept the canon just as it stands, coupled with the open-endedness of the historical approach to the Bible and the recognition of the several factors which go into the shaping of a theology, thus mark a significant move from the approach of the period in which the decision over the canon was made. As a result, the question which we have been considering now becomes a particularly pointed one. Can we, in the light of what we have seen, claim any absoluteness, any unique once-for-allness, in the making of the canon?

The historical consciousness which has now become our possession brings with it also the realization that events, meanings, values in the historical world are all relative. We can see how religious and philosophical beliefs, ethical and cultural values, though considered unconditionally true by those who held them, are in fact rooted in and conditioned by the experience of individual human beings, societies and cultures flourishing at particular times and under particular circumstances. We recognize, too, if we are sufficiently aware, the same influences on ourselves. Therefore without going into the deeper question of whether any absolutes are to be found at all in the realm of religion or morality, or in the claim of Jesus Christ (though this is another question which needs far more discussion), we may at least ask whether the canonization of the Bible was, in this setting, itself an absolute. And put in that way, the question cannot readily be given an affirmative answer.

The arguments which led to the acceptance of the various books into the canon hardly bear a once-for-all stamp about them; indeed, in the case of the New Testament, it has rightly been said that there was a tendency to 'fudge the evidence' on which the place of books in the canon was justified. That is not to say that many of the books which we have had preserved for us on fudged evidence do not deserve their survival; they were rightly preserved for the wrong reasons.[11]

But were they given the right status? As we saw in the first chapter, the Christian Church took over the Jewish Bible without any questioning of this sort at all. But was it correct in doing so? Was not the Jewish conception of the character of the Old Testament perhaps responsible for leading the Church in a direction which it should not have taken? The disadvantages of Scripture as holy and authoritative should be considered, as well as its advantages.

Is it, after all, obvious that the Christian Church was meant to have a holy Scripture in the sense of the Old Testament, which it succeeded in demoting but which it fatally took as a model? It should be granted that the written text is strong precisely where tradition is weak, and that as a fixed text it is less prone to corruption and more capable of acting as a purge, but these need be no more than debating points, as good in their way as the debating points from the other side that it is the Church which decided the Canon and that Scripture does not interpret itself. Is it necessary for them to be blown up into a doctrine of holy authoritative Scripture? It is to be granted also that such a Scripture has effected reform in the Church, notably at the Reformation, though not without grave distortion, for the Reformation was nowhere more disastrous than in its belief that it had achieved a fixed doctrine of the position of Scripture in the Church. Is it to be assumed automatically that what Scripture has done before it will necessarily do again, and that in its make-up it is fitted for this? Has not reform in our own time come from other sources, and included not only reform by the word of God but reform of the word of God?[12]

If the course we have followed has been a proper one, the question 'What about the Old Testament?' has thus turned into an issue of quite central importance. Its consequence has been the raising of no less a matter than the place of the whole Bible in the Church. And again, if the arguments used have been legitimate ones, that place would seem to differ rather from commonly accepted views.

A brief analysis of the factors in Christian theology has prepared us for this position and shown us that it is not so radical in its consequences as might appear at first sight. It may, however, be helpful to point out rather more fully how the Old Testament fits into the general pattern of Christian thinking viewed in this way.

Christian belief takes its distinctive character from the way in which Christians adopt a stand in a particular stream of development, leading from ancient Israel to Jesus Christ and the Christian tradition. Christians look at the world from this perspective, questioning and reinterpreting their position in the light of changing knowledge and experience, including scientific knowledge, inevitably never wholly correct in their insights, but engaged in a constant attempt to clarify them, correct and purify them. The Bible, both Old and New Testaments, has a vital and irreplaceable role in this tradition, witnessing as it does to events and attitudes of central and distinctive importance; but vital and irreplaceable though it may be, it takes its place in the end as one factor among others, itself subject to criticism, revision and reassessment when it is being used to determine present belief and conduct.

But that criticism and reassessment of the Bible can only come if the Bible has been interpreted properly in the first place. This is one of the few ways in which the distinctive character of the continuum of experience can be maintained and Christianity remain recognizably Christianity. It needs its past experience to help to interpret the present, and because that past experience passes back through the New Testament into the Old without a break, the Old Testament must be included, too. We have seen how this interpretation of the past is done, but it is only the beginning, and we must be careful not to exaggerate what we have done or its significance:

> First must come a genuinely historical attempt to understand the kind of men [past generations] were, leading up to the question: 'What must the truth have been and be if that is how it looked to men who thought and wrote like that?' This has to be done over and over again, as we take up the study of successive generations of Christian scholars. We ourselves are in the succession; all we can do is make our contribution from our own point of view, leaving it to be similarly revised by those who come after us. But theology is bedevilled by the illusion that somewhere, sometime, someone really knew the full truth and that what we have to do is to study what he said or wrote, find out what he meant by it, and get back to it.[13]

Thus we do not use our knowledge to show 'what really happened' behind the Old or New Testament account. Rather, we use both our attempt at historical reconstruction and the biblical record together to try to elucidate further the character of the experience of God to which Old and New Testaments lay claim on virtually every page, in order to compare it with our own situation and our own understanding of the nature of our life and our world, and in order to see how God might be related to the world of our experience now.

It would take another book to show more fully how this should not be done and how it might be done; over-simple interpretations of the relationship between past and present abound. One vast field with all kinds of pitfalls for the unwary is the literature which has attempted to see the distinctive feature of the Old Testament in its 'history writing' and has drawn far-reaching conclusions from that. In this survey the category of history and the understanding of the Old Testament as an interpretation of historical events has been deliberately avoided in favour of a rather different approach. Two particular points have been noted where the 'event-interpretation' explanation seems quite unjustified; a comparison of the present book with a more history-centred approach and a consideration of the issues raised might be illuminating.[14]

The important thing is that the interpretation of the Old Testament should be a real attempt at understanding without a premature introduction of our own concerns. In this way it may prove to communicate itself and its understanding more authentically than if we try to bend it to a particular purpose.

If this seems a small contribution for the Old Testament to make, it should be remembered that in this new approach to the Bible the New Testament makes its contribution in very much the same terms, though one step further on. To take up the last sentence of an earlier quotation with a passage from a different context:

> We shall find it hard to accustom ourselves to the uprooting of traditional habits, as hard as it must have been for the compilers of bestiaries in the early seventeenth century. For so long we have taken it for granted that in the New Testament, in the teaching of Jesus, and in the understanding of their faith by St Peter, St Paul, St John and the rest, we have the genuine statement of what Christianity really is; that the subsequent history of the Church is the history of a falling away from the original high level of faith and practice, and that what we need is to get back to the understanding of our faith which those New Testament Christians had. It is hard to get used to the fact that in the sense in which we are seeking it they never had it. They were Jews, most of them Palestinian Jews. They had the outlook of their time, place and culture. Their creed was the Jewish creed of that age. . . . So far from having given us a full and final explanation of the meaning of our faith they were taking the first steps towards its discovery.[15]

All this means that we shall have to follow certain types of argument, particularly those that are heavily orientated towards the past, much further than is often done. Discussion often stops at the point when it reaches 'home ground' in the Bible or arrives at a standpoint that can be labelled 'biblical', as if this were a sufficient resting place. But that is not enough. From this point, arguments still need to be fitted into the wider pattern. More thought, too, will be needed about the significance of listing series of biblical references in support of a statement. Such lists often provide useful comparative material, but if they are also intended to supply authentication of a statement on the grounds that it is paralleled in the Bible, then again further examination will be necessary.

In the light of these considerations, the doubtful quality of much biblical interpretation in 'new theology' will be clear, and even some of the problems discussed in the debates over demythologizing and biblical hermeneutics can be seen to be pseudo-problems. That is not to say that the interpretation of the Old and New Testaments does not raise difficult questions beyond the ones we have looked at; there has been much too little space here to do more than provide some elementary groundwork.

To stop at this point, without going on to discuss the practical questions that this approach raises for the use of the Old Testament in Christian worship, for its bearing on 'devotional' Bible reading may seem to have left out the really relevant questions. But a proper answer to them would require so many other factors to be taken into account that there would be need for another book as long again to do justice to them. In any case, they would take us far beyond the immediate subject of the present study.

Questions like this just cannot be answered by way of an appendix. It is a temptation to think, when compartmentalizing subjects to deal with them conveniently, that practical conclusions can be compartmentalized too. But this is not the case. The questions raised by, say, a discussion about God or the nature of the Church cannot be left aside in thought about the place of the Old Testament in Christian practice; here, again, is an illustration of the complex of factors which go to make up Christian theology.

And this brings us to a last point. Perhaps this approach may seem over-intellectualist and too sophisticated for widespread dissemination. 'The parish will never take it', is a cry which becomes familiar from gatherings of clergy up and down the country. But that is not the main point at issue in the second half of the twentieth century. When the existence of theology as a respectable interest, when its possibility at all is being questioned; when religious belief is regarded as irrational and obsolescent; when communication breaks down, as it so often does, between those who should be presenting Christianity and their potential audience, then it is vital that what is said is reliable, comprehensible and takes its start in a world which can be generally known and verified.

Whatever may not have been dealt with sufficiently in this book, here is a piece of experience which asks to be taken into account when we are generalizing on the whole of human experience, on the nature of our world. Here are facts which need to be taken into account along with other facts; pointers which ask to be taken in conjunction with other pointers which, all together, may give us sufficient pointers towards the viability of the Christian faith as an option, which, in apologetic terms at least, is the most assurance we are ever likely to have.

We have given some answer to the three questions with which this book began: what the Old Testament says, how it says it, and why what it says is important to us. That is as much as the critic can do. After that he must be silent, and against the background which he has set out, leave his subject to speak for itself.

NOTES

1. Adolf von Harnack, *Marcion* (Leipzig, 1921), pp. 127, 222.

2. See T. G. A. Baker, *What is the New Testament?* (London, 1969).

3. For a presentation of the arguments, see J. I. Packer, *'Fundamentalism' and the Word of God* (London, 1958).

4. For a discussion of the relationship of allegory and typology see James Barr, *Old and New in Interpretation* (London and New York, 1966), pp. 103 ff.

5. See R. Bultmann, *Jesus Christ and Mythology* (London and New York, 1958).

6. See e.g. James M. Robinson and John B. Cobb, *The New Hermeneutic* (New York, 1964).

7. Leonard Hodgson, 'Exegesis and Exposition', *Canadian Journal of Theology*, XIII (1967), pp. 43, 46.

8. James D. Smart, *The Interpretation of Scripture* (London and Philadelphia, 1961), p. 190.

9. For further details see John Macquarrie, *Principles of Christian Theology* (London and New York, 1966), pp. 4 ff.

10. Macquarrie, pp. 16f.

11. For further details see C. F. Evans, 'Tradition and Scripture', *Religious Studies* 3 (1967), pp. 323–37.

12. 'Tradition and Scripture', p. 336.

13. Leonard Hodgson, *For Faith and Freedom* (London, 1968²), p. x.

14. Compare, e.g. G. E. Wright, *God Who Acts* (London, 1952); G. von Rad, *Old Testament Theology* (Edinburgh, 1962, 1965); Alan Richardson, *History Sacred and Profane* (London, 1964); with James Barr, *Old and New in Interpretation* (London and New York, 1966) and especially Bertil Albrektson, *History and the Gods* (Lund, 1968), which challenges many current assumptions.

15. Leonard Hodgson, *Sex and Christian Freedom* (London, 1967), p. 41.

For Further Reading

Some general books on the Old Testament (in addition to those mentioned regularly in the notes).

Robert Davidson	*The Old Testament* (Hodder and Stoughton)
Rolf Rendtorff	*Men of the Old Testament* (SCM Press)
John Bright	*The Authority of the Old Testament* (SCM Press)
G. W. Anderson	*The History and Religion of Israel* (Oxford University Press)
J. L. McKenzie	*The Two-Edged Sword* (Geoffrey Chapman)
P. S. Robinson	*A Layman's Guide to the Old Testament* (S.P.C.K.)
James Muilenburg	*The Way of Israel* (Routledge and Kegan Paul)
J. H. Otwell	*A New Approach to the Old Testament* (SCM Press)

Index